# FOUL DEEDS AND SUSPICIOUS DEATHS IN WAKEFIELD

# Foul Deeds and Suspicious Deaths in
# WAKEFIELD

## Kate Taylor

*Series Editor*
**Brian Elliott**

**Wharncliffe Books**

**First Published in 2001 by**
**Wharncliffe Books**
*an imprint of*
**Pen and Sword Books Limited,**
**47 Church Street, Barnsley,**
**South Yorkshire. S70 2AS**

Copyright © Kate Taylor

*For up-to-date information on other titles produced under the*
*Wharncliffe imprint, please telephone or write to:*

> **Wharncliffe Books**
> **FREEPOST**
> **47 Church Street**
> **Barnsley**
> **South Yorkshire S70 2BR**
> **Telephone (24 hours): 01226 - 734555**

## ISBN: 1-903425-07-7

A CIP catalogue record of this book is available from the
British Library

**Cover illustration:** *Assault in a Victorian town court.*

Printed in the United Kingdom by
CPI UK

# CONTENTS

6

# INTRODUCTION

Readers of detective fiction who expect similar mysteries and twists of plot here will be disappointed in these accounts. In real life the murderer and the motive are normally known by the time of the inquest within a few hours of the death. But I hope that there is much else of interest here, not least in terms of the glimpses revealed of the lives of – usually very ordinary – men and women and of how violence and tragedy occur, and in the insights into cultural change.

The research which has led to this book confirms that in the majority of cases the killer and the victim are known to each other, as spouses or partners, or as neighbours or workmates. In other cases the motive for murder is gain and the killing is a consequence of highway robbery or burglary.

Cases of sudden or suspicious death have been the province of coroners since the office was created in 1174. Inquests were normally held, until comparatively recent times, in the nearest public room to the place where the individual had died or the body had been found. Thus the great majority of inquests took place in public houses, where the corpse was viewed by both coroner and jury. The inquest jurors, often guided by the coroner, could bring in a verdict of wilful murder, or manslaughter, and could name the perpetrator(s) of the crime. The coroner would then commit the person(s) supposedly responsible for trial at the Assizes. Prior to 1864 the Assizes for the whole of Yorkshire were held in York but the West Riding got its own Assizes from 1864 and these took place – much to the annoyance of Wakefield people who wanted it there – in Leeds. Under the *Courts Act* of 1971, all trials other than those held before magistrates have been conducted in the Crown Courts which absorbed both the Assizes and the Quarter Sessions.

But how does the historian of 'foul deeds and suspicious deaths' find the material for a book such as this? Local newspapers (the *Leeds Mercury* was founded in 1718 and the first Wakefield paper in 1803) are an obvious source – and this writer has used them extensively – but the task of combing them is a tedious one. *The Times* has a useful index to criminal trials reported in its pages but gives the names of the offenders rather than the places where the offence has been committed. One of the murders recounted here was uncovered when another local historian, Peter Wood, noticed the victim's grave. Another came to light in a bundle of lawyer's papers in the John Goodchild collection. The most important source for this book, however, has been the extensive series of inquest notebooks kept by Thomas Taylor, coroner for the Honour of Pontefract from 1852 to 1900, deputy county coroner for the West Riding of Yorkshire in 1855 and from 1861 to 1864 and county coroner from 1864 to 1900; these are now held by the West Yorkshire Archive Service.

I was fascinated to find, in Mr Taylor's records, the immense number of inquests on dead infants. Infanticide may well have been common but, as Thomas Forbes noted in his essay 'Crowner's Quest', it was easily concealed: 'Found dead' was a frequent verdict, with no further questions asked. 'Overlaid' and 'Suffocated' were again typical verdicts but with the assumption that the death had been an accident. Unless a doctor was able to say that a baby's lungs had been inflated, there was a tendency to regard the newly-born baby as 'stillborn'. I found many cases amongst Taylor's records where no medical evidence was called and where the main witness was some local woman who doubled as a midwife and a layer-out; it seemed enough that she described the child as clean and well cared for up to the time of its sudden death. Again Forbes notes that it was not unusual for a woman to claim that she had given birth standing up and that the baby had fractured its skull as it dropped to the floor.

Forensic evidence became increasingly significant at inquests and trials in the nineteenth century. The practice of dissection may have been established by the early seventeenth century since it seems to have been taken to America by early settlers, but the first record of a post mortem examination in this country comes in 1635 when William Harvey dissected one Thomas Parr. From the seventeenth century coroners began to demand more medical evidence and by the nineteeth century there was increasing reliance on autopsies as a means of distinguishing natural or accidental death from suicide or homicide. The importance of blood grouping was not really recognized, however, until the 1930s. There is a case here, of 1884, where, despite the killer bearing ample traces of his victim's blood, the evidence was regarded as no more than circumstantial, whereas in 1965, when blood was found on some trousers of John Spencer, it could be clearly identified as of a different blood group from the person he had been suspected of killing.

Coroner Taylor's inquest books contain the evidence given at inquests into many colliery fatalities. Frequently the verdict is 'accidentally killed' although today we might want to consider much more closely the degree of negligence involved. But I have included one episode here where a verdict of manslaughter was brought against one of the young victims of an explosion.

We tend to think of the Victorians as dealing harshly with crime but, whilst at the beginning of the nineteenth century we find young men being hung for theft, this book records a number of remarkably lenient sentences for manslaughter later in the century and even an instance of the jury being invited – by the counsel for the prosecution – to bring a verdict of guilty of manslaughter rather than of murder. Feminists may be provoked at the evidence of sympathy for, and indulgent treatment of, some of the men who killed, or seemingly contributed to the death of their wives.

Is Wakefield a particularly wicked place? A number of cases here show that there were parts of Wakefield – and most notably New Street and the surrounding area – where acts of violence were almost commonplace in the second half of the nineteenth century. Ignorance among the inhabitants of the same area could also result in death, as in the case noted here where a baby who was only a few days old was given opium to pacify him. Then three of the murders recounted here took place in the West Riding Pauper Lunatic Asylum, and a fourth was committed by a recently discharged patient. Women, as well as men, were imprisoned in the House of Correction (later to be better known as Wakefield prison) until well into the twentieth century, and some of them had their babies there; not all the babies survived though no charges were brought in regard to the somewhat suspicious deaths described here. As an industrial area, at least from the eighteenth century, the Wakefield district had a considerable population of the working class and it was principally among this strata of society that manslaughter and murder were to be found.

I am greatly indebted to John Goodchild, M Univ, for the advice and information he has given me whilst I have been working on this book and for guiding me in the direction of primary sources. Staff at Wakefield Library Headquarters and at the Wakefield premises of the West Yorkshire Archive Service have been unfailingly helpful and my one visit to York Minster Library was a most happy occasion. My thanks are due also to Brian Elliott, the General Editor of this series, for his encouragement and advice and to the staff at Wharncliffe Books.

## Chapter 1

# Murders Medieval
## 1275-1383

ome few references to murder in the Wakefield area are to be found in the published volumes of the Wakefield Manor Court Rolls. The unique series of records begins in 1274. It details the transfers of land and the pursuit of debts handled by the Courts Baron and the misdemeanours brought before the Courts Leet. Generally speaking the latter courts dealt only with such relatively minor matters as people's failure to scour their ditches, mend their hedges, ring their pigs or keep the causeway in front of their property in good repair, but it also dealt with their engaging in fights, distinguishing between beating and drawing blood. The grave offence of murder was the business of the county Assizes. However on 9 June 1275 the court held in Wakefield heard that Richard Pykard had been killed in the town of Normanton the previous Christmas. It was not known who had done the dreadful deed but suspicion had fallen on Robert, son of Adam Wymes, of Staynford who had been standing near Richard at the time, and it was urged that he ought to answer for it. The court decreed that he should be arrested but a further court on 29 June was told that Robert had not yet been found. We know further from the rolls that Richard had been married to one Juliana and that he had a servant named Alkoc.

It was reported to the court again on 9 June that Elias, son of Thomas Spyal, had killed Roger de Wyrunthorpe at Stanley but that he had fled to the Liberty of Ripon and escaped arrest.

In 1286 Agnes de Scholbrok complained that Richard de Gomersale had killed her husband, William. He denied the offence but was committed to the Assizes at York.

A court held in Wakefield on 11 November 1349 was told that William son of William de Thornes had 'feloniously killed' Robert de Thornes at Thornes on 1 June and that he was in

**Figure 1.** *Normanton's medieval church.*

**Figure 2.** *Normanton's medieval cross, now surmounted by a lamp-post.*

prison at York. A Robert de Thornes had appeared at the Court Baron earlier in the year, on 3 March, seeking repayment of a debt from John Flachard, and on 5 May he brought a further suit against William Wolf, again for debt. On 26 May he was pursuing Thomas son of Richard Wright through the court for payment of wages of 5d.

Fourteenth century records for York Castle reveal the acquittal at the Assizes in 1318 of Adam, son of Philip de Castelford, on a charge of causing the death at Wakefield of John, son of Simon Hodelyn, and the acquittal of Roger de la Rode who had also been indicted for a death at Wakefield.

Further acquittals were obtained by Margaret Aleyn and her daughter Agnes, Thomas Aleyn and Robert de Mora all of whom had been accused by Isabella of causing the death, at Thomas Aleyn's house in Wakefield, of her husband Godfrey de Staynton.

Thomas Taylor, a long-serving nineteenth century coroner for the West Riding, transcribed coroners' rolls from the second half of the fourteenth century. These include inquests in 1358 on Robert Schyloyg, killed at Stanley by John de Flanshaw, James Tewer, killed at Wakefield by Thomas Gotte of Wakefield, and William de Gilkes, again killed at Wakefield by Robert, son of John Meggeson. All three assailants were said to have fled. Gotte was, the coroner noted, abetted by William Pollard.

Taylor transcribed a more detailed case of 1367 when, according to the charge brought by his widow Matilda, John Whiteheued of Sandal was set upon and killed by a group of people at Lofthouse. Foremost among these was Stephen de Kilvyngton, described as a 'co-brother' of the Abbot of Kirkstall, who struck Whiteheued on the head with a Florence sword. Kilvyngton's servant, John, thrust an arrow into Whiteheud's heart. Meanwhile Agnes Colet and Margaret de Baghill added to the victim's injuries by stoning his head.

Not all villains fled. When Henry the son of John the son of Thomas de Wakefield killed Thomas de Yorkshire in 1368 at Wakefield with a cudgel, he gave himself up immediately to the township constable. It was noted in the record that he had been abetted by Robert the son of Thomas Doweston, John Sele, Thomas the son of John Megson, Robert de Penereth, and John de Flockton.

In one unfortunate episode in 1383, a three-month-old child, Juliana Maggs, died at the hand of Thomas the son of Henry de Weinthorp when she received a blow on the head which had been intended for Robert Bull.

## Chapter 2

# Tried for Witchcraft
# 1650

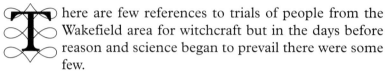here are few references to trials of people from the Wakefield area for witchcraft but in the days before reason and science began to prevail there were some few.

Margaret Morton of Kirkthorpe was brought before York Assizes in 1650 accused by her neighbours of harming – even killing – their children. Her accusers were Joanne Booth of Warmfield and Frances Ward of Kirkthorpe. Joanne said that Margaret had come to her house and given her four-year old son, then in good health, a piece of bread. The child had subsequently sickened, his body had become swollen and his flesh wasted to such an extent that he could not stand. Joanne suspected Margaret of bewitching the boy and sent for her. Margaret then asked the child's forgiveness three times and Joanne drew blood from her with a pin. After that the boy recovered. For good measure Joanne added a couple of other accusations – that sometimes she could not get butter when she churned and that her cheese-making sometimes failed.

Four women, including the witness Frances Ward, examined Margaret and found two black spots, similar to warts, between her thighs. This seemed to them proof of her evil. Margaret had, she said, long been suspected of being a witch, as had her dead mother and sister. She referred to two children who had died in the area two years earlier from a sickness that baffled the community. One of them had said, before he died, 'Good Mother, put out Morton'.

Happily for Margaret the jury was not impressed by the evidence and she was acquitted.

Another accusation of witchcraft was made at York in 1656. Richard Jackson, the tenant of Bunny Hall, Wakefield, accused Jennet Benton and her son, George, of bringing harm to

**Figure 3.** *Houses in the village of Kirkthorpe, 2001*

himself and his family. The issue arose after Jackson had ordered his servant, Daniel Craven, to keep the Bentons off his land. Confronted by Craven, George Benton threw a stone at him which cut his upper lip and broke two of his teeth. Craven brought an action against Benton and obtained satisfaction. But Jennet Benton then threatened Jackson, saying that it 'would be a dear day's work' to him or those close to him before the year was out.

Jackson claimed that since Jennet had 'cursed' him, his wife had become deaf, one of his children had had fits, he was himself racked with pain, and he had lost eighteen horses and mares. Moreover Jackson claimed to be woken in the night by strange noises of music and dancing or of bells. One night three heavy groans had been heard, causing the dogs to howl. The account is given in Lupton's *Wakefield Worthies* but there is no indication there of whether the Bentons were ever tried.

## Chapter 3

# A Most Barbarous and Cruel Robbery and Murder 1677

On the night of 6 December 1677 Anthony Wilson and his wife were subjected to torture by a gang of thieves who took what they could from the house and left Anthony himself dying from a knife wound.

We do not know exactly where the Wilsons lived, only that it was in a small village near Wakefield and that Anthony was a prosperous tenant farmer. The event is told in an eight-page pamphlet published shortly afterwards in London under the title of

**A full and true relation of a most Barbarous and Cruel Robbery and Murder committed by six men and one woman near Wakefield in Yorkshire.**

The violent robbery was described as - *the most horridest and wickedest Robbery and Murder that hath ever been heard of for many years.*

It was in the middle of the night that the six men and a woman broke into the house, carrying lights in their hands and with 'vizards' over their faces. Anthony Wilson and his wife were bound and gagged before the villains turned their attention to their two daughters, lying in a 'trundle-bed' under that of their parents. They too were bound and gagged. Next the two male servants, occupying another room, were treated similarly and finally the maid, found in another chamber, was also bound and gagged.

The gang then returned to the Wilsons' room and, ungagging Anthony, demanded to know where his money was. He assured them that he had only six pounds in the house, having just paid a half year's rent to his landlord. He gave them the key to his trunk which stood beside the bed. They swore, however, that 'they very well understood that he had far greater

**Figure 4.** *The* Three Houses Inn, *Sandal, in 2001, near to the original* Three Houses *where John Nevinson was arrested.*

sums in the house which they must have before they went'. One of them lit a match and held it to Anthony's fingers 'until such time as it had burned all the flesh from the bone'. But

Anthony had no more to say. He was gagged again and the thieves turned to his wife, treating her to the same torture, holding the match to her fingers, so it was said, for a full quarter of an hour. They then rifled the bed-chamber taking what money there was, linen, clothing and a silver bowl. They were about to leave when the woman thief 'who of all others is the most cruel' tried to persuade her comrades to murder the whole family 'for fear they might afterwards come to the knowledge of them and procure the law against them'. The men, we are told, were of a 'little better nature' or else they 'were not willing to add murder to the horrid crime of theft'. So it was the woman who took a knife from her bosom 'and thrust it into the body of the man (Anthony) leaving the good man to wallow in his own blood'.

And so the helpless family lay for the rest of the night as the thieves made their escape. At seven the next morning a thresher came to work in Anthony's barn. Finding it, most unusually for that hour in the morning, still locked up, he went to the house, and, gaining no response to his knocking, went in and up the stairs. He swiftly undid the gags and bonds and then went into the village to alert the neighbours. They gave what assistance they could, we are told, but 'there never being a surgeon near they could not get help for the good man before such time as he bled himself to death'.

The pamphlet comments that up to the time of printing the villains, supposed to live somewhere nearby, had not been found.

It may well be, however, that they were the gang of John Nevison, or Nevinson, a notorious highwayman who was ultimately arrested at Sandal in March 1683 and who was executed at York in May the following year. Evidence was given at the Assizes against Nevison and his five associates (Edmund Bracy, Thomas Wilbore, Thomas Tanherd, John Bromett and William or Robert Everson) by the woman member of their gang, Elizabeth Burton. She provided examples of ten of their exploits but she did not refer to the theft and murder at the Wilsons. Perhaps it was she who carried the fatal knife.

## Chapter 4

# Death of a Low Abusive Fellow 1788

The survival, in the John Goodchild collection, of a lawyer's brief prepared for the Lent Assizes at York in 1789, allows an account to be given of the circumstances that led to innkeeper Thomas Burnell being charged with causing the death of Samuel Womersley, described in the brief as a 'low abusive fellow' and as 'some sort of quack and commonly called the dog doctor'.

Burnell kept the *Saw Inn* in Little Westgate. In the yard of the inn, which ran down to George Street, was a Key Alley - perhaps something like a bowling alley - and on 11 August 1788 Burnell was playing keys with a number of others when Womersley came up the yard to the gate to the Alley and gave Burnell 'some foul scurrilous language which much exasperated him', hailing him with, 'Damn thee, eightpence a pint'. Burnell threw a key at him, though it missed its mark, and, when Womersley continued his invective, Burnell seized him and forced him to the ground. 'If he struck a blow,' the lawyer, David Colvard, said, 'it was to his head'.

Womersley was able to get up, although he needed the aid of the yard wall for his first steps, and then to walk upright out of the yard and into Westgate. It seems that his shoulder was dislocated, however, and later the same day he called on blacksmith John Birkett who manipulated it back into place. A few days later Womersley complained to a magistrate that he had been assaulted and Burnell was 'taken up by his warrant for battery'. He offered compensation for the injury and the two settled for the sum of two guineas plus Womersley's expenses.

It was not until 15 August that Womersley thought it necessary to see a doctor. He then sent for William Mitchell

**Figure 5.** *The* Saw Inn, *Westgate, in the mid-twentieth century.* The John Goodchild Collection

who attended him the following day and 'thought him not in any danger, bled him and saw him no more until after his death'.

Lawyer David Colvard commented that Womersley walked about daily and seemed in no great pain. On 18 August he walked downstairs as usual and was able to go out of his door, and he ate with a good appetite. Then he sat in his chair and died.

Mitchell examined the body – though without conducting an autopsy - and said that he 'found a cartilage at the extremity of the sternum depressed' but could not say whether this was

---

## SAW - INN, Wakefield.

# TO BE SOLD,

### ( By Auction )

### At the SAW - INN, in Wakefield,

### On the 3d of May 1792,

*Betwixt the Hours of 6 and 8 in the Evening,*

*(Unlefs before difpofed of by Private Contract) fubject to Conditions,*

ALL that Freehold MESSUAGE, TENEMENT, or INN, known by the Sign of the SAW, ftanding on the South-fide of *Weftgate*, the principal Street in *Wakefield*, near the Centre of the Town, and now occupied by Mr. *Thomas Burnill*; together with the Cottages, Outbuildings, Garths, and Folds, thereto belonging ; and all thofe Pieces or Parcels of LAND, extending from the faid Inn, to the *Ings-Lane* there, occupied as Gardens, by feveral Perfons as Undertenants to the faid *Thomas Burnill*, and all Rights and Appurtenances belonging to, and now occupied with, the Premifes.

The LAND, divided into Gardens, ftands in a moft eligible Situation for building upon, and might be formed into an entire Street, to communicate from the Top of Weftgate to the Ings-lane.

There is a good Pew in *Wakefield Church* belonging the Premifes.

The Tenant will fhew the Premifes ; and other Particulars may be had of Mr. SCOTT, Upholfterer, or of Mr. COLVARD, Attorney at Law, both in *Wakefield*.

---

**Figure 6.** *Advertisement for the sale of the* Saw Inn *in 1792.* The John Goodchild Collection the result of a blow or not. The inquest was held the same day, before the coroner Richard Linnecar, and the verdict was death by the 'visitation of God'. The coroner and Mitchell agreed that there was no evidence of a blow to the body. The following day the body was swollen 'by putrefied air' but an 'eminent Wakefield surgeon' said that that often happened following a death from natural causes.

Nonetheless Burnell was arrested on a charge of manslaughter and committed by the magistrates for trial at the Assizes. He was either found not guilty or given a very modest sentence for an advertisement for the sale of the *Saw Inn*, by Burnell's landlord, in 1792, shows him still there and ready to show prospective buyers around.

## Chapter 5

# A Struggle in the Snow
# 1788

A gravestone in Sandal churchyard and a brief report in the *Leeds Mercury* of 30 December 1788 are all that remain to bear witness to the murder of John Matthewman, the seventy-year old servant of William Beatson of Hollingthorpe, near Wakefield.

Matthewman was also a tanner and had lived in Hollingthorpe for fifty years. On the morning of 23 December he left home about five o'clock in the snow to ride to Leeds market. In Hollingthorpe Lane he was waylaid and beaten with a weapon which fractured his skull, making a wound so large 'as to contain a moderate sized hand'. His body was then thrown face down under a holly bush. There was evidence of a

**Figure 7.** *The wording on John Matthewman's gravestone in Sandal churchyard: 'John Matthewman of Crigglestone Cliff who was murdered near Hollingthorpe 23rd December 1788 aged 72 years'.* Peter Wood.

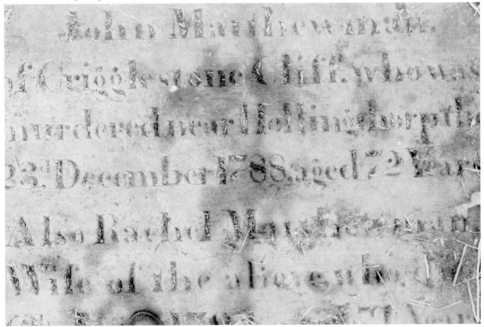

struggle in the snow some yards from where it lay and there was a great deal of blood both on the ground and on Matthewman's clothes. One of the old man's pockets was pulled inside out as though the villain, or villains had been searching for money.

The paper went on to describe the victim as of a 'most excellent character for diligence, honesty and sobriety'.

At the inquest the jury brought a verdict of wilful murder against some person or persons unknown. It seems that the assailants were never traced.

## Chapter 6

# Murdered for the Money for a Cow 1803

When Thomas Terry was hanged at York on 14 March 1803 it was, it was said, the first time that anyone had been executed at York without the conventional hood over his head. Terry had torn it off in a frenzy.

Terry and his associate, Richard Heald, were convicted at York Assizes in March 1803 for the murder of Elizabeth Smith, a sixty-seven year old widow of Flanshaw on 2 September 1802. In his final hours, Terry protested that he had done the deed alone and that Heald, who was being hanged at the same time, was innocent. The two young men, aged about nineteen or twenty, were apprentices, working for Flanshaw handloom weavers Thomas Wilkinson and a Mr Artle.

Widow Smith earned a living by keeping a few cows and selling their milk. But in the summer of 1802 she had had some ill luck: two of the cows had died leaving her almost destitute. According to the Wakefield historian John Hewitt, the widow belonged to a 'cow club' from which she was able to obtain recompense. However a contemporary account reports that it was through the 'human assistance of her neighbours' that she was able to buy one cow and that one of her sons, who lived in Leeds, sent her eighteen guineas to buy another. Another of her three sons, Thomas, lived close to his mother in Flanshaw and he recalled at Terry and Heald's trial, that Heald had pressed him as to when his mother planned to buy another cow. He had also seen the pair at his mother's house a number of times in the weeks preceding the murder.

It was in the small hours of the morning of 2 September that neighbours of Mrs Smith, the Towlertons, were awakened by the sounds of her screaming. Mary Towlerton looked out of the window and saw a man in his shirt sleeves, with a lighted candle, in the widow's bedroom, stooping and looking about, apparently in a great hurry. She woke her father, William, and her brother, John, and they shouted from the window thinking that the man must be the widow's son. But the light being immediately extinguished, the Towlertons raised the alarm. John Towlerton was to say later that he saw a man in a dark-coloured waistcoat and dark apron emerging from Mrs Smith's window. William Towlerton saw someone washing his hands in the trough opposite the house and the water had been left bloody.

Mrs Smith's son Thomas, together with neighbours Henry Glover and John Clarke, went to the house and found the old lady lying on the floor, bleeding and speechless, with a pair of tongs, bent and covered in blood, lying beside her. In the adjoining bedroom was a bloody spade; a candlestick and a razor, both spattered with blood, were on the bedroom table and amongst the bedclothes was the iron part of a 'switching bill'.

Shortly afterwards Terry and Heald arrived on the scene, volunteering to help in the quest for the killer. Heald was actually wearing a dark waistcoat and dark blue woollen apron and Terry had one of his hands bound up.

The pair came under suspicion swiftly. One Anne Illingworth identified the switching bill as hers: she had lent it to Terry's master, Thomas Wilkinson, and it had not been returned. Wilkinson found a bloody handkerchief hidden in Terry's bed. Terry then made a statement to the township constables, Thomas Shaw and Samuel Linley. He and Heald, he said, had planned to meet outside Widow Smith's at one o'clock in the morning. He had assisted Heald to get in by a window and had then followed him. After they had struck several blows at the old woman, Heald had taken a razor while Terry held her head. It was then that Terry's hand had been cut. Terry had gone to the window to see if all was clear and when he got back he found that Heald had dragged their victim into the next room and was 'braying' her over the head with the tongs. He claimed that he had told him to desist.

Shaw found confirmation of a part of Terry's story when he discovered bloodstains on the frame of the window Terry had looked out from; the stains matched, in shape, the injury to Terry's hand.

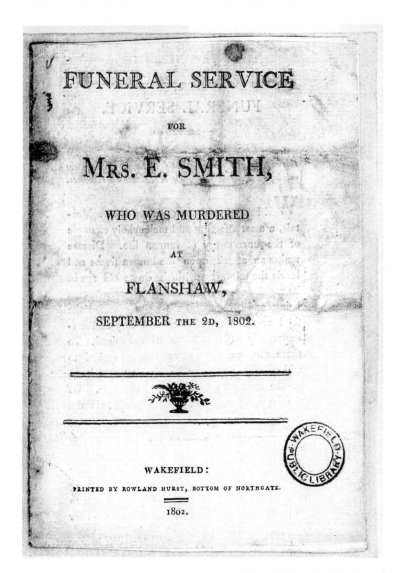

**FUNERAL SERVICE**

FOR

**MRS. E. SMITH,**

WHO WAS MURDERED

AT

**FLANSHAW,**

SEPTEMBER THE 2D, 1802.

WAKEFIELD:

PRINTED BY ROWLAND HURST, BOTTOM OF NORTHGATE.

1802.

**Figure 8.** *The title page of the sermon preached at Widow Smith's funeral in 1802.* Wakefield Library Headquarters, Local Studies Collection.

Heald denied the whole thing. When Terry admitted his part, Heald said, 'I thought thou would not have deceived me so - thou knows I was not with thee'. He claimed that his master could clear him since he was always locked in his room at night. The deputy constable, John Wood, who arrested Heald, had, however, noticed fresh marks on his face and lip as if made by someone's finger nails. It was also obvious that he would have had no difficulty – even with the door locked –

of escaping from his room via the window.

At the inquest into Widow Smith's death, the jury concluded that she had been killed by both Heald and Terry.

The two apprentices were taken to the House of Correction in Wakefield prior to being sent to York. The Taskmaster there, James Wraith, swore at the Assize court that Terry had told him that Heald had persisted for a long time in trying to persuade him to steal Widow Smith's money and that he had heard Heald say, as they beat the old woman, 'Damn her, she has

**Figure 8.** *Widow Smith's gravestone, Westgate Chapel.*

scratched me'. He claimed also to have himself noticed blood on Heald's stocking. Artle's wife said that Heald's apron had had bloodstains on it and that – most unusually – he had washed it. Both men were found guilty of the murder and were sentenced to death.

On the morning of the execution, Terry insisted to the chaplain that Heald was innocent. The chaplain reported his words to the judge but the judge remained convinced of his guilt. He asked his marshall for advice on whether the circumstances suggested a stay of execution to allow for further investigation, but both felt that Terry was now lying.

On the way to the 'drop' Terry was in a state of violent distraction and on the scaffold itself it took five men to restrain him. He cried out that if Heald were hung he would himself be guilty of two murders. The eye-witness who wrote the report for the *Leeds Mercury* said that he seemed sincere but agreed that the evidence given at the trial demonstrated Heald's guilt. Did Terry go 'to meet his maker', as the reporter asked, 'with a lie on his lips'?

Widow Smith was buried in the grounds of Westgate Chapel. A gravestone bears an image of the tongs with which she was beaten.

## Chapter 7

# He Could Not Have Hanged Himself 1804

**W**hen Elizabeth Oldroyd told the Assize court that her son had been with her throughout the morning of 18 July 1804 she must have hoped that she might gain his acquittal. But what she said directly contradicted the evidence she had given at the coroner's inquest into the death of her husband, Joseph. Benjamin Oldroyd was found guilty of the old man's murder and, although the execution was deferred for two months while the judge consulted his fellow judges about points of law arising from the contradictions, he was hanged at York's New Drop on 27 May 1805.

The Oldroyds lived together in a small cottage at Milnthorpe Green, Sandal. They had only two rooms – a living room and a 'parlour' in which were two beds, one for the elderly couple and the other for their forty-five year old son. At the back of the cottage was a small garden with an adjoining cowshed and small croft.

It seems from the evidence of a neighbour, Jane Arnold, at the York Assizes, that there were frequent quarrels between the father and son. Mrs Arnold had heard sounds as though the son were beating his parent and the mother was begging him to desist. Benjamin had said 'Damn thy foul face. I hate to see thee,' and 'I could kill him as freely as I ever eat a bit o' bread'. Benjamin was generally known as a 'bad character' and was seldom seen about during the day but was said to be out frequently at all hours of the night.

On the day he met his death, 18 July 1804, Joseph Oldroyd had been seen at 4.30am by another neighbour, William Jagger, in his usual health. Joseph and Elizabeth had gone together to their croft to milk the cow. According to Elizabeth's original evidence, Joseph had complained of feeling unwell and she had returned to the house with him and seen him to bed.

Back in the house she had found their son bleeding from a cancerous sore on his neck and the left part of his face. This bleeding, apparently a regular occurrence, drove him, she said into paroxysms of rage. Leaving the two men in the cottage, she had gone into the garden to pick currants, spending some four hours at the task. She had then gone back indoors and called to her husband asking him whether he felt well enough to take some breakfast, but there had been no answer and Benjamin told her that Joseph had gone out.

Elizabeth said that she then searched for Joseph in the cowshed, the croft and at the watering place at the top of the croft but found no sign of him. Back at the cottage Benjamin said he was faint from bleeding and would go out to pick a cherry. A moment later he called out 'Mother, Mother, I have found my father dead in a fit'. She ran out and saw Joseph lying dead with his head against the cherry tree, with one end

**Figure 10.** *Cock and Bottle Cottages, Manygates Lane, formerly the* Cock and Bottle *public house where the inquest into the death of Joseph Oldroyd was held.*

of a cord round his neck and the other fastened to a branch of the tree. Benjamin removed the cord although she had told him that nothing should be touched until the coroner had seen the body. Benjamin said it would be better to say nothing about it.

It was then, according to Elizabeth, about twelve noon. She and her son simply left the old man lying there until six in the evening when two neighbouring women, Sarah Jagger and Lucy Kay, were summoned to lay out the body. According to Sarah, Elizabeth had said, 'I was getting currants when this happened. If I had been in the house at the time, I could have prevented it. It's so sudden a thing. Folks will say we have killed him.'

William Jagger helped to carry Joseph into the house and later gave evidence that he had discovered cord marks on his neck, bruises on his back, clotted blood in his mouth and part of his tongue hanging through his lips almost bitten through. The surgeon who examined Joseph's body confirmed the marks of a twisted cord on his neck; his windpipe had been dislocated and the carotid artery was ruptured. There were severe bruises on his back and thighs which could have been caused only by a violent struggle against some hard substance. The immediate cause of death was strangulation.

Elizabeth and her son insisted that Joseph had hanged himself. But the inquest jury thought differently and Benjamin was committed for trial at York. When Elizabeth went to Wakefield on 25 July to sell her fruit, she was assailed by a number of women in Kirkgate who threw her fruit into the street and drove her out of town.

At the Assizes Elizabeth claimed that, on the morning of his death, when her husband returned from the milking he had offered to show her where he kept the key of his box, telling her that she did not know how soon she would want it. Joseph, she said, had already made several suicide attempts. Contrary to her statement at the inquest she affirmed that after her husband had taken to his bed about 8am, her son went with her into the garden and the pair stayed out for two or three hours until the time they both discovered that Joseph was missing.

But Mrs Arnold's evidence was supported by another

neighbour, Thomas Coldwell. He spoke of Benjamin's brutality towards his father and the abusive expressions he had used. Neighbours affirmed, too, that in the past Elizabeth had admitted to being afraid that Benjamin would kill his father and that she had said that, when the bleeding fit was on him, he would seize his father and utter imprecations. But the most telling piece of evidence was that Joseph simply could not have hanged himself. The bole of the tree was a mere four feet in height and there was no branch of sufficient strength to bear his weight. The bark of the tree was unmarked.

A search after Joseph's death brought to light a calf collar hanging on the back of the parlour door with two iron links and a short piece of cord which appeared recently cut. Among a quantity of other head collars was a piece of cord about two yards in length which corresponded with the piece attached to the iron links. Clearly Benjamin had both the means and the opportunity to murder his father.

To the last Benjamin protested his innocence. Before his execution the chaplain invited him to pray but he refused, saying that it was wrong to kill an innocent man. He had to be dragged from his prison cell by force and was so 'unruly' on the platform of the 'drop' that the executioner was obliged to 'turn him off' very swiftly. His body was sent to Leeds for dissection.

## Chapter 8

# The Consequences of Dissolute Behaviour, 1821

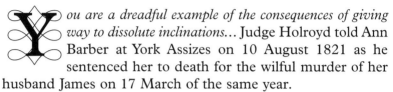*ou are a dreadful example of the consequences of giving way to dissolute inclinations...* Judge Holroyd told Ann Barber at York Assizes on 10 August 1821 as he sentenced her to death for the wilful murder of her husband James on 17 March of the same year.

Barber, whose maiden name was Smirthwaite, was forty-four and the mother of three children, the first of them by a previous husband. She was described as 'a very ordinary looking woman' but it seems clear that she killed her husband in order to marry her lover, William Thompson.

Some little time before the murder, Barber had left her home at Royds Green, near Rothwell, to live with Thompson in lodgings at Potovens. When the landlord discovered that the couple were not man and wife, he had turned them out and the pair had gone back to Royds Green to live under the same roof as James. Whilst he seems to have accommodated the situation, his neighbours were aghast and their protests had led to Thompson's being ejected.

On the eve of his death, James Barber had been suffering from a heavy cold and his wife, pretending to comfort him, had roasted an apple for him and given him a glass of warm, sweetened ale to wash it down. When ultimately Ann Barber confessed, to Reverend W Flower at York Castle a short time before her execution, she admitted that the ale had been well laced with arsenic. James died in agony. A neighbour who dropped in on the evening of 17 March urged Ann to send for a doctor, reminding her that there were three living within a mile of her home. She resisted the idea saying that no good could be done for her husband and he would be dead by morning. In fact he died about four o'clock the next morning, a Sunday. Ann was promptly arrested by George Wadsworth, the constable. An inquest was opened the following day and the two doctors who had carried out a post-mortem examination said that they had found a considerable quantity of arsenic in James's stomach. The jury demanded further investigation. The next day their foreman, the coroner Christopher Jewison, and Wadsworth compelled Ann to dress in the clothes she had worn the previous Friday when she had gone into Wakefield. She was taken to the shops of two druggists, Lawton and George Brydges Reinhardt who had moved to Wakefield from Leeds in 1804, purchasing a business at the top of Westgate. The latter not only recognised her but could swear to her buying a pennyworth of arsenic on the Friday when she had explained that it was to kill mice.

At the Assize hearing Mr Hindle, a Rothwell surgeon, confirmed that he had found the lining of James's stomach badly corroded and inflamed and that he had verified the presence of arsenic by 'the usual tests'. The lungs had been blackened, consistent, he said, with mineral poisoning.

Ann's brother, John Smirthwaite, and her sister, Elizabeth Richardson, testified to her hard-working disposition and good character. Her youngest daughter, Jane, 'a pretty and interesting little girl,' was too upset to give evidence.

Ann was asked whether she was pregnant – which would have allowed a respite until the baby was born – but she was not and she was executed three days after the trial. The charge against her was one of 'petit treason' as well as murder. This charge related to the killing of a person to whom the murderer owed allegiance – a servant killing his master, or, as here, a wife killing her husband. The sentence for this involved not only death by hanging but also the drawing of the villain upon a hurdle before the public gaze from her cell to the scaffold. Ann was so drawn at 11.30am but the distance was a short one. She then joined in a short service and, as the cord was passed round her neck, was heard to say, 'O Lord Jesus, I am a-coming to thee'.

## Chapter 9

# Murdered for Twenty Shillings Worth of Silver, 1824

Poor Jonathan Depledge, a sixty-eight year old blacksmith who lived in a cottage at Newton, just outside Wakefield, never recovered from the injuries he received at the hands of three good-for-nothing lads who robbed him on the evening of Thursday, 30 September 1824 as he was walking home.

As he passed St John's Church, at about seven o'clock, he had met the three youths and wished them good evening. They had not replied and he had gone on his way towards Newton Bar. But then the youths had attacked him, covering his mouth and pushing him to the ground. They had beaten him on the breast with his own stick, searched his pockets and taken his money, and then run off.

One Samuel Lockwood came upon Depledge, looking very ill, and helped him home where the old man was able to tell Ann Hudson, a neighbour who assisted him in the house, what had occurred. The lads had stolen all his money – two crown pieces, three half-crowns, two shillings and a sixpenny piece, amounting in all to twenty shilling or one pound in value. Dr Ebenezer Walker was called to attend Depledge the same evening and found him in great pain. He had difficulty in breathing. He died some ten days later and Dr Walker said at the inquest that death was due to internal bleeding and inflammation of a lung.

The jury brought a verdict of murder against persons unknown.

However they did not go unknown for long. Thomas Hudson, son of the landlord of the *Spangled Bull* public house at Newton recalled three young men eating mutton chops and drinking ale at the *Spangled Bull* on the afternoon of 30 September and having seen the same young men about seven

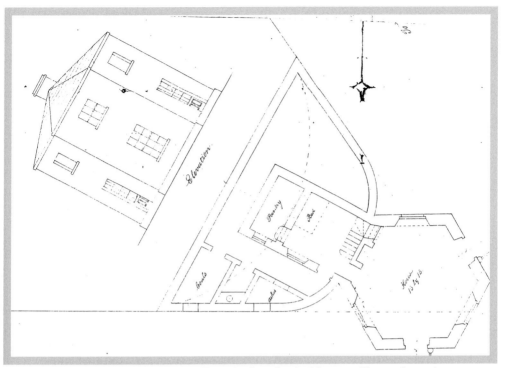

**Figure 11** *Architect Charles Watson's plans for the Newton tollhouse, drawn in 1805.* The John Goodchild Collection.

o'clock the same evening near where Depledge had been attacked. Three youths of the same description had stayed at the *Butcher's Arms* on both 29 and 30 September and on the latter evening one of them had changed a crown piece there. They had left Wakefield on 1 October on the Booth Ferry coach. Within days of Depledge's death his attackers had been identified, arrested in Leeds and brought back to the House of Correction in Wakefield. In fact one of the three, Robert Moseley, had been released from the House of Correction only two months previously after serving two years' imprisonment there.

Moseley and his companions, seventeen-year old Benjamin Morrill and Joseph Sharp, who, like Moseley, was twenty, came before the magistrates at Wakefield Court House on 15 October where a full confession by Sharp was the central evidence of their guilt. All three were committed for trial at the Assizes and were sent to York Castle.

Newton bar house itself, where sixty-seven year old Edward Ellis was the keeper, had been the site of another outrage earlier in the same year. About 9.30pm on the evening of 8 March, shortly after the mail coach had passed, there was a cry of 'Gate' and Ellis's wife, Martha, opened the door to attend to what she assumed were passers by. She was knocked down as four young men, dressed in rough fustian jackets, rushed into the house. One held her down while two others beat her husband breaking two of his ribs. The men then made off with six silver teaspoons marked M E J, a silver watch made by Trentham of Liverpool, £15 in silver and some £100 in bank notes. The Ellises had both a good fire and candles and Edward claimed to have taken good note of his assailants and to recognise them as labourers who had been brought to the toll house on a number of occasions by Mr Ward, the lessee of the Leeds and Wakefield turnpike tolls. Two of the villains, Morris Camfield and Michael White, both natives of Ireland and Roman Catholics, were tried at York in August. Both were said to show the utmost contrition and perseverance in imploring for mercy from God. They were hanged at 12 noon on 29 November on a scaffold behind York prison and were interred in the Castle burial ground. Their accomplices were named as Timothy Conolly and Matthew Fitzpatrick.

## Chapter 10

# Killed while Looking for Work
# 1828

T hanks to the public spiritedness of local people, the murderer of eighteen-year old William Longhorne, or Longthorne, was swiftly identified. Bringing him to trial, however, took rather longer.

Longhorne, whose home was at Barmby Moor, near Pocklington, had been employed as a stable boy and had experience of driving a chaise, but in October 1828 he was out of work. He tramped first to York and then to Wakefield. On Thursday, 16 October, as he passed through Aberford, he fell in with a Wakefield lad named William Mosey. The two walked on together and when they reached Wakefield, Mosey directed Longhorne to a lodging house kept by Elizabeth Wraith in Warrengate. Later in the day, a girl – subsequently identified as Mosey's sister – called at the Longhorne's lodgings with a message that 'someone' wanted to speak with him. Evidently this was Mosey himself, and he and Longhorne arranged to set out the next day for Ferrybridge. The pair left Mrs Wraith's about six o'clock the following morning.

Later that morning Longhorne was found alone, crawling through a field called Water-doles, near Snydale, bleeding profusely. His throat had been cut almost from ear to ear. His windpipe was severed and the root of his tongue was almost cut through. He was taken to the *Cross Keys* public house in Snydale where Dr Robert Buchanan of Loscoe Grange and Dr Joseph Thompson of Pontefract shared the task of stitching his wounds. They held out no hope whatever of his survival and he died at about eleven o'clock the following morning.

Between Longhorne's being found and the inquest the following Monday, ordinary local men and women had clearly been busy. A labourer, Robert Cockill, traced Longhorne's route to a brook over a beck separating Snydale and Aketon.

**Figure 12.** *The* Cross Keys, *Snydale, where William Longhorne died.*

**Figure 13.** *A modern bridge close to the site near Snydale where William Mosey cut William Longhorne's throat.*

He found signs of a scuffle, plenty of spilled blood and also a bloodstained razor.

Longhorne could not speak but he could write on a slate and make gestures and he remained, it was reported, 'perfectly sensible' until his death. He could thus give his horrified carers his name. He was questioned first by the vicar of Normanton, Reverend Robert Hodgson, and was able to tell him where he had come from and that he had been attacked by his companion. But he had no knowledge of Mosey's name. Cockill sat up all night with the poor lad and drew more information from him. He was able to confirm that the assailant had worn a blue and white striped smock and a hairy cap. He was also able to indicate how much money had been stolen from him.

A cloth-dresser from Alverthorpe, Benjamin Mallinson, found a bundle close to Featherstone Church containing a waistcoat, two pair of stockings, a shirt marked with the initials W L and two handkerchiefs. When Thomas Lee held the inquest the bundle, as well as the razor, were produced as exhibits. The bundle was identified by Mrs Wraith as being Longhorne's. But Mrs Wraith had more to tell Coroner Lee: she had recognised Longhorne's visitor as Mosey's sister and knew that Mosey's parents lived in a yard off Warrengate. Longhorne had told her that he was going to walk to Ferrybridge to seek work there. Moreover William Mosey had called for him early on Friday morning.

A series of witnesses gave evidence of having seen Longhorne with a man answering Mosey's description - in a blue and white smock with a hairy cap - at various points on Friday morning: William Farrar, a gardener from Eastmoor saw the pair in Warrengate about 6.15am; Samuel Day, who lived near Fall Ing Foundry, saw them going towards Heath about 6.20am; Robert Watts, the township constable, who lived at Snydale, saw them crossing fields at Warmfield about 7.00am; a little after that Grace Quarmby, of Featherstone, had seen them going across Warmfield Green; Benjamin Mallinson, who had left Alverthorpe at 6am, saw the two young men near Snydale windmill; he had dallied, picking hips and the pair had gone ahead of him; when he reached the footbridge over the beck he had seen the blood.

The jury had no difficulty in giving a verdict of wilful murder against Mosey who was said to have been seen on the Great North Road near Ferrybridge.

Longhorne was buried in Normanton churchyard and a collection was taken at the following Sunday's service to provide a headstone for his grave. His father attended the funeral.

But Mosey remained on the run. Again the general public sought to be helpful in reporting sightings of him and a wholly innocent young man who bore a superficial resemblance to him was arrested at Kendal. It seems, however, that Mosey was never apprehended.

## Chapter 11

# Recognized by a Missing Toe
# 1846

It was not easy to recognize James Macdermot almost five years after the murderous attack in which he was implicated but a key witness knew that he had had a serious injury to a toe and a police officer was able to confirm that one of the toes of the man before the magistrates had been amputated.

Macdermot was one of a group of five Irishmen who attacked Henry Skelton and his two companions in New Street, Wakefield, as they made their way home to Stanley on the night of Saturday 14 March 1846. New Street, which ran eastwards from Westmorland Street, and the yards which led from it, had for decades a most unsavoury reputation. It was said at the time of the attack on Skelton that it was 'infested by a party of Irishmen' and that 'few persons are allowed to pass unmolested'. Almost as rough was the parallel Nelson Street.

The other two men, named Green and Ward, managed to escape but Skelton was knocked to the ground, kicked and beaten. He had been in Wakefield to attend the market and a meeting of his lodge – perhaps the lodge of a friendly society. He was attended by Dr Benjamin Kemp but he died from his injuries on 13 May.

Witnesses – one of them the son of the landlord of the *Foresters Arms* – were able to name two of the attackers and the inquest, held at the *Woodman* public house at Stanley, ended in a verdict of murder against twenty-two year old John Sharon, or Shearon, and forty-year old Luke Haukon, or Harkon 'and others'. Shearon and Haukon were tried at York Assizes in December 1848 and were found guilty of manslaughter. They were each sentenced to ten years' transportation.

But who were the others? Robert Lockwood, a labourer, was sure that one of the group was a man nicknamed Paddy who

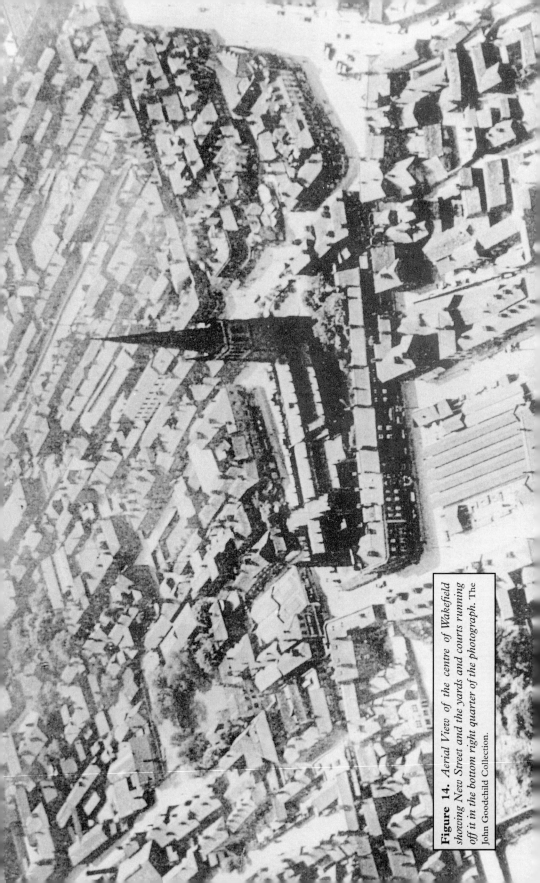

**Figure 14.** *Aerial View of the centre of Wakefield showing New Street and the yards and courts running off it in the bottom right quarter of the photograph. The* John Goodchild Collection.

had, a short while before, been going about on crutches and who said he had lost a toe when some scaffolding dropped on him when he was working on the new building at the House of Correction.

After Skelton's death, Macdermot, who had lived in Nelson Street at the time of the attack and was working in Wakefield as a labourer, collected his wages and left the town. This was, itself, enough to give rise to suspicion, and then – although like so many other Irishmen – he was known as Paddy. Stupidly, at the end of 1850 he returned to Wakefield. He was swiftly arrested and brought before the magistrates in January 1851. But Macdermot had aged in the intervening years and although William Clayton, a keeper at the West Riding Asylum who had witnessed the attack in 1846, was sure this was a man he had seen then, Robert Lockwood was much less positive. Macdermot was sent for trial at York Assizes on a charge of manslaughter on the evidence of his missing toe.

At the trial, on 11 March 1851, the defending barrister argued that Macdermot had not been identified clearly as one of the attackers. However he was found guilty and, like his associates, got a sentence of ten years' transportation.

## Chapter 12

# The Penalty of a Filthy Trick
# 1858

few beers and a few lads with too little to do and the consequences can be dire. Certainly they were in 1858 for railway pointsman Samuel Carter and his victim, twenty-five year old railway labourer Edward Dunnill.

The events which led to Dunnill's death in January 1858 occurred on a Monday in the previous July.

A group of young men working on the railway line at Normanton gathered together in the shunter's box to have some beer. One of the men, Charles Hanby, left the box to urinate and Dunnill took the breakfast can belonging to Carter and held it under the stream. When Carter returned to his box about 3.00pm and discovered what had happened he challenged Dunnill and then seized a poker and dealt him a blow which felled him and knocked him senseless. William Craven, another of the group, helped him home to Altofts where he lived with his mother.

Dunnill was able to return to work after some three weeks and one of the witnesses at the inquest, held at the *Ship Inn*, Altofts, reported having seen him cleaning out some drains on the York line at Normanton at that time. But Dunnill was now prone to heavy bleeding from the nose. On one occasion he assisted the landlord of the *Talbot* by lifting a beer barrel and this brought on a considerable haemorrhage.

In early September for the first time Dunnill saw a doctor, the Altofts surgeon, William Fowler because of the recurring bleeding. Dr Fowler continued to attend him but Dunnill's health worsened from the loss of blood, and the haemorrhages continued. He died on 25 January.

At the inquest, Dr Fowler said that a post-mortem examination had revealed a fracture above Dunnill's eye and damage to the ophthalmic artery. He believed that the injuries would have been caused by a blow from a blunt instrument. The jury reached a verdict of manslaughter against Carter.

Carter, who was twenty-four, was tried at York Assizes on 9 March 1858. He was found guilty and sentenced to three years' penal servitude.

## Chapter 13

# A Fracas at Whitwood 1860

T*he village of Whitwood has acquired a most unenviable reputation in consequence of the violent fracas which are continually occurring there*, announced the *Wakefield and Halifax Journal* in November 1860 when just such a violent fracas had led to the death of forty-two year old coal miner Joseph Wilkinson and a charge of manslaughter against his neighbour, twenty-five year old Edward ('Long Ned') Hirst. Both men worked for the local colliery company of Henry Briggs, described by the same newspaper as providing 'almost exclusively employment for the inhabitants who are generally speaking illiterate and depraved'.

Wilkinson, who certainly had a reputation for being quarrelsome, lived with his wife and thirteen-year old daughter, Sarah, in a row of cottages close to the line of the North-Eastern Railway. Some three weeks before the disturbance, Hirst and his wife had moved into another of the cottages three doors away. All the cottages had plots of garden at the front but a footpath to an adjoining field ran across Hirst's plot and had been regularly used until he moved in. His closing the path led to the quarrel.

On Saturday, 24 November, after Wilkinson had returned from work, he and his wife went out at about 4.20pm to buy provisions at Castleford market. They had done their shopping by 6.00pm but Mrs Wilkinson had left her husband behind at Aaron Sidwell's beer house. She and her daughter waited up for his return. He came along the waggon road some time between midnight and 1.00am, roaring drunk, shouting and singing. But instead of going straight into his house, he took the path across the Hirsts' garden, telling his wife that he was going into the 'cloise'.

The inhabitants of the various cottages seem to have stayed

**Figure 15.** *The* Mexborough Arms, *Whitwood, where the inquest into the death of Joseph Wilkinson was held.*

up late! Hirst claimed later that he was just trying on a pair of new boots when Wilkinson arrived.

Martha Robinson, a dressmaker from Lofthouse who was staying with another neighbour, William Crossland, provided an account of what happened next, at the inquest on Wilkinson which was held the following day at the *Mexborough Arms*. She had been standing at Crossland's door and, as it was a light night, had, she declared, seen everything. Hirst, who, Martha said, was wholly sober, advised Wilkinson to go home, asserting that neither he nor anyone else was to come onto his premises. Wilkinson refused and had gone up to the Hirsts' window and began abusing Mrs Hirst. She came out with a hoe and attempted to attack Wilkinson with it. He wrested the hoe from her and refused to give it up. As Hirst struggled with him to gain possession, Wilkinson fell to the ground. Thereupon Hirst seized a piece of rail and struck Wilkinson violently two or three times on the head. Hirst and his wife then retreated into their house.

Elizabeth Wilkinson, the miner's wife, confirmed that she and her daughter had then stepped across to Wilkinson, who was lying on his face, and that, as she tried to turn him over, her hand had sunk into the wound on his head and been covered in blood. She and the girl had turned to her next-door, Samuel Hyde, for help, but he simply went back into his own house leaving her and her daughter to get the injured man into their house as best they could. The doctor had been summoned and Mrs Wilkinson had gone out to look for the local policeman. PC Banks had been on duty that night. He had heard Wilkinson singing as he went home, but had continued his beat to Whitwood Pottery and Methley Bar. Meeting Mrs Wilkinson on the way back, who told him that her husband had been 'chopped' by 'Long Ned', he had hurried down the railway line to the cottage. After the doctor arrived he had searched the Hirsts' garden and found both the hoe – covered in blood – and the bloodstained broken rail. There were prints of both shod and bare feet on the ground. Wilkinson had died about 2.00am and PC Banks arrested both the Hirsts and took them to Wakefield where Superintendent Hall charged them both with murder.

Samuel Hyde told the inquest that, although there had been quarrelling between Sarah Hirst and Wilkinson's sister-in-law, he knew of no previous altercation between Hirst and Wilkinson, however he had seen Hirst stike at Wilkinson that night 'with a stick'.

An adjourned inquest on 29 November heard from a surgeon, Ebenezer Walter Kemp, that Wilkinson's death was the result of a blood clot on the brain caused by one of the blows to his head.

The jury brought in a lesser verdict of manslaughter against Edward Hirst, leaving his wife free. He was committed for trial at the Assizes.

When the case was heard at York in December, the question was raised again as to whether the fatal blow had actually been struck by Mrs Hirst with the hoe but the notion was dismissed. Hirst was described there as a man who was normally quiet and industrious and he had, it was said, expressed great remorse. He was sentenced to four months' hard labour.

## Chapter 14

# Twice Exhumed
# 1860

Frances Adamson, a sixty-three year old spinster of independent means, lived quietly at Milnthorpe, Sandal, as a tenant of the cornmiller, J J Cartwright, in a house she shared with Thomas Wood. The two had known each other for fifty years and had shared a home for seven. They had separate rooms but were both looked after by a resident general servant, Emma Stringer, who had been with them for two years and was twenty-three at the time of Miss Adamson's death on 15 August 1860. A cleaning woman, Hannah Bateson, also helped in the house.

Until May 1860 Frances had been attended by Dr Edward Waddington but for the last few months of her life she had called in Dr John Hirst, a surgeon, farmer and maltster, of Boyne Hill.

Frances, whose brother was a clergyman of the Church of England at Padiham, had converted to Roman Catholicism and worshipped at St Austin's in Wakefield. Her change of faith had led to a breach with her family.

Frances was taken ill on 2 August with vomiting and diarrhoea. Dr Hirst had been called in and for a few days she seemed to recover. Then there was a recurrence of the malady on 8 August. Dr Hirst last saw her alive when he visited twice on 14 August but had then no notion that she would shortly die. However she died at 5.00am the following morning. Emma, one of her sisters, and Hannah Bateson were all present. Death was certified by Dr Hirst as being due to peritonitis and Frances was buried in Wakefield Cemetery.

But then the rumours started. Emma, gossips said, had fabricated a will in which Frances was supposed to have left her her clothing and personal adornments. On the day of her death, Emma's brothers had removed trunks from the house in

At the Graziers Inn Sandal Magna on Saturday the 8th day of September 1860 on

Frances Adamson decd (adjd. from 3rd inst:)

Thomas Nunneley of Leeds F.R.C.S.E. ...

... Last thursday week I had a jar given to me by my son John Albert who informed me that he had recd from Superint Hall. I opened it last Saturday night & found a very small portion of red colored fluid, a very small portion of the larger curvature of the stomach, a small piece of the large intestine & a little bit of the liver. & that evening started to analyse. The operations proceeded for several days. The stomach was red - There was nothing remarkable in the appearance of the portions. I tested them for poison and particularly for mineral poison - I hand in my report dated the 7th inst:

which contains my opinion and is as follows

"Sir                    Leeds September 7th 1860.

I have now proceeded with the analysis so far as the materials at my disposal have permitted me to do - I regret as I intimated to you might not improbably be the case, I am unable to arrive at a demonstration satisfactory to my own mind. On the little fluid there certainly was no trace of poison and in the gut the indications were so slight as fairly to be regarded as negative but with the portions of the stomach and liver the result has been different - From them I have obtained indications so suspicious that could I have operated on larger portions so as to have been able to vary the experiments and thus exclude every possible chance of error and still have obtained the same result I should have spoken without hesitation but as the portions sent to me have not been sufficient to furnish the means for so doing and it is of the utmost importance in such investigations

**Figure 16.** *Pages from Thomas Taylor's inquest book recording a part of the evidence into the death of Frances Adamson.* The John Goodchild Collection.

not to arrive at an opinion until every possible source of error has been excluded, and the value of one set of tests been corrected or confirmed by another mode of manipulation I can only recommend that the body be re-exhumed when there ought to be no difficulty in obtaining sufficient of the viscera to submit to such a series of experiments as can leave no doubt of the absolute correctness of the analysis - This course I think more prudent than at present giving an opinion which more complete examination might possibly shew to be hasty by explaining what now appears to be suspicious and which if correct the course I suggest would certainly be required to confirm -        I am Sir

Thomas Taylor Esqr     Your faithful Servt
   Coroner                Thomas Nunneley
                           F.R.C.S.E."

Adjourned to Wednesday the 26th inst: at 6 p.m. - Jurors bd. in £10.

At the house of Correction Wakefield on Monday the 10th day of September 1860 on view of the body of

Thomas Wade decd

William Wood of Wakefield M.D. sw says I am Surgeon to the W.R. Prison - Decd was 43 years old & a General Dealer. He also went by the name of Wright & also of Marshall. He was convicted of uttering a Counterfeit half crown & sentenced to 12 Calr months hard labor from the 17th May last. He was committed here on 2nd May last. He was then healthy. He was mat making at first but soon afterwds complained of his stomach & head. He was sent into the garden to work but still complained & I observed a defect in his speech. I sent him to the Hospital on 21st July last & general paralysis came on gradually. He died this morning between 3 & 4 oclock. He was properly attended to. He was quite helpless.

William Wood M.D.

a milk-cart. Emma was already selling some of Frances's things. It was, surely, strange that Frances had died in the end so suddenly. The finger of suspicion fell on the poor servant.

An exhumation was ordered because of the 'several strange and mysterious circumstances shrouding Miss Adamson's decease'. It took place on 23 August. The body was removed to the *Graziers Inn*, Agbrigg, which stood next to the cemetery, and an inquest was opened there the same evening. It was adjourned so that a post-mortem could be carried out by Dr Waddington. When the inquest resumed on 29 August it was a very serious affair with C B L Fernandes representing the dead woman's family and Joseph Stringer, a Horbury solicitor, representing Emma's interests.

Dr Waddington said that he had found no trace of poison in the body. The cause of death was clear – a perforated ulcer which had caused peritonitis. But the jurors raised many questions and were clearly not satisfied. It seemed that Dr Waddington had removed and retained some of the deceased's internal organs. The jury wanted an expert in toxicology to analyse them. Thomas Nunneley, a surgeon of 22 Park Place, Leeds, was asked to undertake this but he claimed not to have enough material to examine and requested a further exhumation. Poor Frances was disinterred again on 19 September.

Some idea of Nunneley's findings reached Superintendent Hall of the Lower Agbrigg division of the West Riding Constabulary, before the resumption of the inquest on 25 September and he obtained a warrant for the arrest not only of Emma but also of her sisters, Matilda, who was twenty, and Abigail, aged fifteen.

At the inquest itself on 26 September Nunnely claimed to have found traces of arsenic throughout the body, notably in the spleen, liver, kidneys and brain, consistent with it have been ingested over a long period. Asked whether he realised that ladies were in the habit of taking arsenic to improve their complexions, Nunnely rejected the notion. However John Taylor, of Mountain and Taylor, chemists, said that Frances had been a customer of his and had been supplied with arsenic from time to time since 1856. She had also bought vermin-killer.

**Figure 17.** *The* Graziers Inn, *conveniently close to Wakefield Cemetery, where the inquest into the death of Frances Adamson was opened.*

Emma and her sisters came before Thomas Holy Holdsworth JP on 29 September and were remanded in custody. On 3 October they appeared again. Emma, it was said, sat quietly and calmly, her face covered by a veil. Her sisters were discharged. Emma's counsel did all he could for her. It was established that Frances regularly dosed herself with all manner of 'quack' medicines and that her appearance was consistent with her taking doses of arsenic. It was suggested that Nunneley was not sufficiently competent and that Dr Waddington had found no arsenic present. Mr Wood lived in the same house and had the same meals as Frances, yet he had not been taken ill.

It was to no avail. Emma was committed for trial at York Assizes.

The Assizes opened on 9 December. The Grand Jury

included a number of the leading Wakefield gentlemen. There was John George Smyth MP, of Heath, Sir Lionel M S Pilkington of Chevet Hall, Edmund Calverley of Oulton, James Milnes Gaskell, MP of Thornes House, Richard Monckton Milnes MP of Fryston Hall, and Edmund Waterton of Walton Hall. It was evident from his opening address that Mr Justice Hill was concerned about the case. He referred to two pending trials each of which, he said, required 'special attention'. The second was that of Emma Stringer. There was, Hill said, conflicting evidence as to whether Miss Adamson had died of poison at all, and, whilst he granted that Emma had a motive, there was only 'loose' evidence that there had been poison in the house or that Emma had had possession of it.

The case came before the court the following Thursday, 13 December. No evidence whatever was offered and Emma was discharged!

But did she do it?

## Chapter 15

# Left to Die
# 1862

Neighbours' fear and the inability (or perhaps lack of effort) of the Relieving Officer, Thomas Whitaker, to obtain help, may very well have contributed to the death, in wretched circumstances, on 1 June 1862 of fifty-one year old Sarah Bainbridge in a slum dwelling at Greenhill, Eastmoor, Wakefield. There was evident dissatisfaction, too, with the doctors who had attended her.

It was the responsibility of the Relieving Officer, under the Poor Law, to ensure that any necessary provision was made, albeit modest, for the poor and infirm. The cost of relief was borne by the ratepayers. Whitaker, then aged sixty-one, had been in his post for five years. Prior to that he had worked as a lime-burner and brick-maker.

Sarah had in the past worked in a worsted mill and also as a charwoman. She had only recently moved to Greenhill where she lived with her brother, Mark Bainbridge, and her ten or eleven-year old daughter, Ann, the child of a relationship with one Frank Dyson. She was already suffering from valvular heart disease when, three weeks after the move, she fell ill with typhoid fever.

On Friday, 23 May she took a note from the Relieving Officer to William Pitts, the assistant to Dr Thomas Walker, in order to obtain medicine. The following day Dr Walker himself visited her. He advised her to stay in bed. On Monday and Tuesday Williams Pitts visited her. There seemed to be no food in the house, she was too ill to do anything for herself and her brother, who also had a fever, was too ill to help her. On Wednesday Pitts went himself to the Relieving Officer's home. Sarah was too ill to be moved to the workhouse, he said, and she needed a nurse urgently. She should have tea, gruel, rice and sago and she needed someone to make these for her.

He reported the situation to Dr Walker who went to the house with Pitts the following day. It was clear that Sarah was extremely ill. She was lying on a make-shift bed on the floor upstairs and the house was, in the doctor's words, 'in a lost state'. Pitts spoke to some of the neighbours, accusing them of allowing her to 'die like a dog'.

Pitts called in again on Friday and found Sarah still in the same pitiful condition. She had had neither food nor medicine since his last visit. He sought help again for her from the neighbours but they said that she was a stranger and they were afraid of catching the fever themselves. He then went again to ask Whitaker to get a nurse. At some point on Friday Mary Blackburn of Primrose Hill visited Sarah, although not at Whitaker's instigation, and washed her, re-made her 'bed' and gave her some of the medicine. She later gave her opinion that it was 'improper' for Sarah to be left unattended. On Saturday evening young Ann went to Pitts for more medicine and he gave her a note to take to Whitaker, who lived on Park Lodge Lane, insisting that Sarah needed an attendant day and night.

It was on the Saturday, too, that a neighbour named Holdsworth reported the appalling situation to Wakefield's Chief Constable, James McDonald, who sent one of his officers, Inspector William Burton, to the house the same evening. He was sufficiently shocked at Sarah's state to go directly to see Whitaker. Sarah clearly had tried to get a nurse but no one would go to the house. Burton went directly back to McDonald and the two visited the house together at 11pm. By then Sarah was dead. McDonald himself reported her death to the coroner.

At the inquest the jury members were appalled at what they heard. The foreman, who happened to be also a councillor, said that it seemed Sarah had been starved to death. They wanted to know why Dr Walker had not obtained nursing care. He was put on the defensive but insisted that he had not thought his intervention necessary as he had had Whitaker's promise that he would find a nurse. The jury proposed to return a verdict that she had died from heart disease and typhoid fever aggravated by want of the necessaries of life and necessary attention. The implications of such a verdict clearly

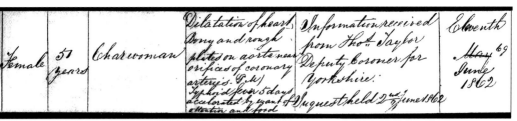

**Figure 18.** *A part of Sarah Bainbridge's death certificate giving the jury's verdict that her death was 'accelerated by want of attention and food'.*

concerned the coroner, Thomas Taylor; he pointed out that it would be a criminal offence if death had been hastened by neglect of professional duty, and the inquest was adjourned to allow for a second medical opinion.

When it resumed, at the *Griffin Hotel*, the following Tuesday, a lawyer, W H Banks, was present to look after the interests of the Relieving Officer. Dr Walker tried to insist that, because Sarah had a heart condition, typhoid fever would under any circumstances have proved fatal; he was not prepared to say that she would have lived longer if she had been properly attended to and he insisted that she had not died of starvation, but he did agree that she should never have been left unattended. Whitaker seems to have made no effort to obtain proper nursing care. Perhaps he was afraid of spending the ratepayers' money. He spoke of approaching some of the local paupers, who received 'out-relief' and whom he might have thought were under some obligation to the Board of Guardians, but they claimed to be too ill or too infirm to undertake nursing. But Whitaker should have looked elsewhere; the Chief Constable argued that, provided a fair payment was offered, there was no difficulty in finding a nurse. The jury asked that Dr W R Milner, surgeon at Wakefield prison, be sent for and questioned him closely about whether, if she had been adequately cared for, Sarah would have recovered. The most he was prepared to say, however, was that nursing did have a considerable influence on the chance of recovery and that her life might have been prolonged with better nursing. The coroner then advised the jury that before anyone could be regarded as culpable, the negligence must be 'unreasonable' and must amount to 'gross' negligence.

The jury persisted in its verdict and Sarah's death was deemed to be due to heart disease and typhoid fever 'aggravated by want of proper attention and necessary food'. Sarah's death certificate records that she died from 'dilatation of the heart, bony and rough plates on aorta near orifices of coronary arteries, and typhoid fever accelerated by want of attention and food'.

Dr Walker commented at the inquest at the unhealthy nature of dwellings at Eastmoor. There was a lack of drainage and the ashpits and privies were foul. When he first saw Sarah he recognised that she was suffering from 'dirt' as well as disease.

The Board of Guardians met the following week to consider Whitaker's actions. He was told firmly that people must be properly looked after. They had met during the time that Sarah was so ill and they demanded to know why Whitaker had not reported the case to them then. The matter did not rest there. The Guardians asked the Poor Law Board to conduct an investigation and a month later the poor law inspector, J Manwaring, held an inquiry. It was emphasised that Whitaker had instructions from the Guardians to provide nursing care when it was needed. Dr Milner again stressed the importance of good nursing. Whitaker admitted that from the Wednesday to the Friday, whilst Sarah lay dying, he had not even looked for a nurse. 'I might not have taken so wise a course as some, but I acted to the best of my judgment,' he declared.

Sarah's brother, Mark, died six days after Sarah, again from typhoid fever. As for young Ann – she went to the workhouse.

## Chapter 16

# The Baby Never Stood A Chance
# 1863

With an alcoholic mother and a violent father, newly-born George Haigh never stood a chance.

The mother, Ann Haigh, had been living with her mother, Elizabeth Storey, in Sloop Yard, Kirkgate, Wakefield for three months when George was born on 30 March 1863. Her husband, Walter, lived in Horbury but it seems that the couple could neither get on together nor bear to be long apart. Both frequented the *Spotted Leopard* public house in Kirkgate although Sarah Ann Clarke, who served there, had sometimes refused Ann entry because of her drunken state.

Six weeks before the baby was born, Ann and her husband had been drinking together and arrived back in Sloop Yard in quarrelsome mood. Walter had struck Ann and, after she had fallen into the ash-place and got up again, he banged her head against the wall. Despite the altercation, the pair spent the night together. No doubt there were many other similar episodes.

It seems that Walter was not the only person to injure Ann. On 27 March, when she had been out with one Rachael Lockwood, she had been hit by a Charles Crossland. Then on 28 March she was turned away from the *Spotted Leopard* and, either from anger or the effects of drink, or both, she had thrown herself down.

On 29 March, a Sunday, she was at the *Spotted Leopard* again with her husband, there was a fracas and again Walter knocked her about.

Ann had made arrangements with a local widow, Mary Broadhead of Ingwell Yard, to attend her confinement. The day after the latest tiff, Ann obtained 3d worth of rum from the *Spotted Leopard*. That evening Mary was called in to the Sloop Yard house and delivered little George about 10.30pm. He had, Mary later said, a black mark over his right eye and his left hand was swollen. He died the following evening. When Sarah Clarke called at the house later that evening, she found its grandmother nursing the dead child on her knee.

Dr Ebenezer Walker was called in. The baby was a seven-month child, he decided, and had died because it was both premature and debilitated because of the violence that Ann had suffered.

At the inquest on 2 April, the jury were inclined to allocate the blame a little further. A verdict was finally decided that little George had died of debilitation because of his premature birth but whether this was in consequence of his mother's course of life or of violence to her, the evidence was not sufficient to show.

## Chapter 17

# More Dead Babies
# 1863-75 and 1946

Little Ann Cook was already toddling when she was imprisoned with her mother Margaret, at Wakefield gaol on 5 August 1863. Indeed, on the day she admitted the pair, the prison matron, Martha Ann Burden, had rebuked Margaret for letting her child run around on the cold flags. Margaret's answer was as chilling as the stone floor. She could easily spare the child, she said, as she had plenty more at home.

Margaret was the wife of a Sheffield man, John Cook, who was a fettler in an iron foundry.

During the next three weeks, the baby was with Margaret the whole time. As far as the prison authorities knew, the child was healthy and the mother had no physical disabilities, although it seemed to Mrs Burden that the woman was entirely indifferent to her child. No one had visited them and Margaret had received no letters.

On the evening of 28 August Margaret reported that she had had three epileptic seizures during the day. It was the first mention she had made of being prone to fits. The following morning she got up as normal when the bell rang and went at 6.15am to empty her slop bucket. However, when the assistant matron, Ann Featherstone, went to Margaret's cell at 6.30am she found the baby lying dead. Margaret said that she had had to get up in the night to walk about in the cell with the child and had had another fit. When she got up in the morning she thought the baby was simply asleep.

Dr William Wood, the prison surgeon, examined little Ann and was able to say that she had died of suffocation but that he could find no external marks of violence. An inquest was held the same day at the *Black Boy Inn* in Westgate. The verdict was simply that Ann had died of suffocation but whether accidentally or not there was not sufficient evidence to say.

## 1864

Edward Binks was less than two weeks old when he died in Wakefield workhouse. He was the child of twenty-one year old Maria Binks of Alverthorpe, an unmarried mother, who had been employed in a worsted mill and later had gone into service. When she was first pregnant she had evidently gone back home to her parents, William Binks and his wife, but – presumably when they became wise to her condition – she was turned out and had spent the four months up to 22 February 1864 sleeping rough and working as a charwoman.

On that day Maria had gone into labour. She was found sitting at the roadside in Alverthorpe by Susannah Kirk, the wife of a coalminer. Susannah and one Charles Issott helped Maria to her father's gate but he refused to take her in. Instead he asked an Alverthorpe labourer, John Jessop, to take her in his cart to the police station and then to the workhouse. Neither Maria's mother not her father went with her.

On the journey it became clear that the birth was imminent. The assistant to Dr Horsfall, the medical officer to the workhouse, which was in Park Lodge Lane, attended to Maria in the cart as it made its way up Warrengate and the baby was born before they reached the workhouse door.

Dr Horsfall himself attended mother and child the following day. The baby was rather small – an eight-month child, Dr Horsfall thought – but it seemed to be alright for a day or two. It then began to refuse food. It died on 5 March.

An inquest was held at the *Butchers Arms* when both Susannah Kirk and John Jessop gave evidence. Their criticism of Maria's parents was clear. Dr Horsfall reported briefly on his findings after a post-mortem examination. He found no marks of violence on the body and gave the opinion that Edward had died because of the debility occasioned by premature birth. The verdict was one of natural causes.

## 1865

When Emily Jennings was discharged from Wakefield prison on 25 September 1865, her four-week old baby, Henry, had

**Figure 19.** *The former gate of Wakefield Prison, in Love Lane, with the governor's house to the right and one of the prison wings in the background.* Wakefield Historical Publications.

seemed healthy. A few hours later the child was dead.

Emily was a metal-spoon rubber, employed in Sheffield. She was committed to prison in June 1865 and the baby was born there on 27 August. Martha Shaw, matron at the prison, said that Emily seemed a good mother and treated the child kindly.

Emily was unmarried but had a close relationship – there is

no means of knowing how close – with her father who lodged in Wakefield during her imprisonment. Her father met her as she came out of prison at 8.15am. The pair went first to his lodgings and then set out to walk to Oakenshaw Station, Walton, to catch a train for Sheffield. Little Henry suckled at Emily's breast as they went, wrapped under his mother's shawl.

At Agbrigg railway bridge, at mid-day, they paused for a moment and it was then that, according to her evidence, Emily looked at the baby and found it was dead. She and her father went to a nearby house, home of Elizabeth Illingworth, where, Elizabeth said, Emily 'fret very much'.

An inquest was held the same afternoon at the *Jolly Sailor* public house, Agbrigg, when the verdict on Henry was 'accidentally smothered'.

### 1874

Emily Tolson was also unmarried when she fell pregnant in 1874. At the time she gave birth, she was living at Flushdyke with her aunt and her aunt's husband, Joseph Illingworth, a woollen manufacturer. Emily, who was nineteen, helped her aunt in the house and also worked as a burler for her uncle. She gave birth alone in her room at the beginning of November. It is very possible that her family were unaware of the pregnancy. In struggling to deliver the child it seems that she fractured its jaw. It lived, Dr John Greaves Wiseman thought, for no more than an hour.

At the inquest at the *Commercial Inn*, Ossett, on 2 November, it was recorded that the child, who was unnamed, died from a fracture of the jaw caused by the mother trying to facilitate delivery when alone.

### 1946

The killing of 'secret' babies is a perennial human tragedy. There can be little more sad than a mother killing her new-born child. Usually the girl, or woman, is unmarried, gives birth in secret, and is bewildered, with nowhere to take the child and fearful of being found out, perhaps also of losing a job.

In May 1946 a newly-born boy child was found in a

shopping bag in a locker at Pinderfields Emergency Hospital which had been established during the second world war. He had been strangled within fifteen minutes of birth. The mother was a twenty-four year old nurse, Peggy Burrows, from Stapleford, Nottinghamshire. The case of infanticide was heard at the West Riding Assizes at Leeds in July. Peggy – by then Mrs Burrows – was given a three-day sentence and, since she had already been imprisoned for longer than that, was discharged immediately. She and Burrows had known each other for seven years but he had been unaware of her pregnancy.

The above are just a very few of the many cases where inquests were held in or near Wakefield on dead babies. How far deaths were really accidental or how far the mothers were actually to blame we shall never know.

## Chapter 18

# No Preparations for the Baby 1864

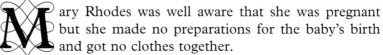ary Rhodes was well aware that she was pregnant but she made no preparations for the baby's birth and got no clothes together.

Mary, the wife of farm labourer Joseph Rhodes, was separated from her husband and lived at the home of Mrs Scott, in Bond Street, Wakefield, where she was the cook. The couple already had two children, the older one aged seven. At Mrs Scott's, Mary shared a bed with the housemaid, Elizabeth Jagger, and had told her that she was expecting a baby although she did not say when. She threatened to kill Elizabeth if she told anyone. She added darkly that there was no point in getting clothes as the child would not live. She kept her condition from Mrs Scott.

On the morning of 5 August 1864, Elizabeth got up at her customary time of 5.00am to find Mary kneeling on the floor. The baby was born a few moments later. Mary asked Elizabeth to cut the umbilical cord for her but she felt unable to assist and gave a pair of scissors to Mary to do it herself. Without tying the cord, Mary wrapped the baby in a flannel petticoat and laid it on the bed. By 6.00am both she and Elizabeth were downstairs going about their normal tasks although Mary managed to slip out to the privy to throw the afterbirth away. At 8.45am Mary went back upstairs and called to Elizabeth to join her. By then the baby was dead and the petticoat was soaked in blood.

Mary suggested that they should ask James Craven and his wife, Ann, who lived at Eastmoor, to bury the baby and they should tell no one else about it. She had known Ann since the days when she worked at the 'College School' where Craven was a gardener. Mary urged Elizabeth to get permission from Mrs Scott to go out so that she could call at the Cravens.

**Figure 20.** *Bond Street, Wakefield, where Mary Rhodes worked for Mrs Scott and where her newly-born baby bled to death.*

No evidence was given as to quite what happened next but clearly Mrs Scott became aware of the situation later in the day and reported it to the police. As a consequence Mary was interviewed and arrested. She was taken to the police station and given the care and attention that she needed.

At the inquest at the *Royal Hotel* in Wood Street, on 6 August, Doctor Ebenezer Walker gave evidence of examining both the dead baby and Ann at Mrs Scott's in the presence of the Chief Constable, James McDonald. The birth was, in his view, a 'full-term' one and the child weighed six pounds and was eighteen inches long. When he saw it, the baby was clean and was wrapped in linen but the umbilical artery protruded from its abdomen and it had clearly bled to death. An autopsy revealed that the internal tissue and the baby's organs were very blanched from lack of blood. A petticoat covered in blood was found soaking in a pail.

The jury brought a verdict of manslaughter against Mary and she was committed to prison in Leeds. The case came before the Assizes only a few days later, on 18 August. The judge explained to the jury that they had to decide whether Mary had deliberately set out to kill the child, had been guilty of gross negligence in not tying the cord, or had acted out of ignorance, in which case they could accept that the child had died of natural causes.

They were drawn to the last explanation and Mary was found not guilty.

## Chapter 19

# Killed with a Shovel
# 1865

When, on 28 November 1865 Jonathan Waite told asylum attendant James Kimpton that he would show him something that would astonish him, Kimpton can hardly have expected the horrific sight that met his eyes. Lying between two beds with his face smashed was forty-two year old William Burran, a woolcomber by trade, who had been admitted to the West Riding Pauper Lunatic Asylum in 1852, discharged in 1859 and re-admitted in 1863.

**Figure 21.** *One of the men's dormitories at the West Riding Pauper Lunatic Asylum.* The Stephen Beaumont Museum.

There was a good deal of blood on the carpet.

When Kimpton had gone a little earlier to the ward kitchen to fetch some beef tea, Burran had been engaged in bed-making in the dormitory and Waite had been sent to get a bucket and brush to clean out the single rooms. When Kimpton came back through the day-room he found Waite in an armchair. Waite led him to the body and showed him the shovel he had used in the attack. It was one that was normally kept in the bucket room off the dormitory. By eleven o'clock, when all the morning chores were done, it would have been locked up.

At an inquest at the asylum the following day a verdict of wilful murder was brought against Waite and he was removed to the House of Correction. Waite was twenty-three and a tailor by profession. The case came before the West Riding Assizes in Leeds on 19 December but, as the reporter for the *Wakefield Express* noted, his 'appearance when placed in the dock left no room for doubt that he was insane'. The asylum medical officer, Dr John Cleaton, gave evidence to that effect and it was accepted that he was not fit to be tried. The judge ordered that he be detained during His Majesty's pleasure.

## Chapter 20

# She Could Not Read the Label
# on the Bottle, 1866

Nineteen-year old Frances Snowden, sister of the general-store keeper Edward Thompson and sometime assistant in his shop, could not, as she put it, 'read so well'. Had she been literate Mahala Learoyd might have lived for a few more years.

The widowed Mahala, who was seventy-five, lived near Wakefield at Lee Moor, Stanley, with her nephew Benjamin Bulmer and his wife, Mary. She had a weak heart and when she felt unwell she was in the habit of taking a little tincture of rhubarb, some nitre and some oil of almonds. She obtained these by sending the Bulmers' daughter, nine-year old Emma, to Thompson's shop close to the common.

On Monday afternoon, 30 April 1866 Mahala gave Emma two and a half pence to get some tincture of rhubarb. Thompson was out and the shop was closed but Emma found Frances Snowden in the yard behind it and the two went into the shop by the back entrance. Emma pointed out the container to Frances who measured out an ounce, putting it in a small bottle.

Later that afternoon Mahala's son, Squire Learoyd, a railway platelayer, dropped in to see her. Whilst he was there, Mary measured out some of the tincture and gave it to Mahala in a cup of tea. Within fifteen minutes Mahala said that she had never felt so ill in her life. Mary exclaimed, 'Surely yon lass has not given her the wrong stuff'. She showed Squire what was left in the bottle and as soon as he had tasted it he asked Mary to give his mother some milk. He took the bottle back to the shop. Frances indicated the container she had filled it from. Edward Thomson, now back there, took it down and showed Squire the label – tincture of Opii, in other words opium. Squire went back to the Bulmers and asked them to give his

**Figure 22.** *Lee Moor in 2001.*

mother camomile tea before he went on into Wakefield to called out Doctor Rayner. Alexander Clement Rayner had regularly visited Mahala. He reached the Bulmers at 9.45pm by which time the old lady was more-or-less insensible. He administered an emetic and also used a stomach pump. He then gave her a pint and a half of coffee via the tube into her stomach. He remained at the house for more than three hours, sprinkling her with water and seeing that she was moved about. But his efforts were in vain. She died in the small hours of Tuesday morning.

An inquest was held the next day at the *Ship Inn* at Stanley. Dr Rayner had undertaken a post-mortem examination and gave his view that Mahala had died of an overdose of opium. Despite the evidence pointing to the innocence of Frances of any vicious motive, the jury gave a verdict of manslaughter against her. The coroner readily allowed bail, however, and when the case was brought to the Assizes at Leeds in August, the Grand Jury chose to ignore the charge.

No doubt Emma was a good little reader but had never got beyond the word 'tincture' in identifying the bottle!

## Chapter 21

# Shooting in a Wakefield Street 1866

homas Kelly, a thirty-five year old Derby man, came to Wakefield in June 1866 with one purpose in mind – to find and kill Leopold Stanton.

Kelly had been in America for two years working in the docks. His wife had written to him regularly but the letters had been sent from a wide range of places. She explained this in her correspondence by saying that she was travelling with a 'lady' who was selling lace.

When Kelly returned to his home on 19 May his wife was there but local gossips told him that it was a man that she had gone away with, not a woman. Mrs Kelly denied this at first but Kelly found letters from her lover who was indeed a traveller in lace but was Leopold Stanton.

Kelly was bent on seeking the man out and exacting revenge. When he learned that Stanton was in Wakefield, he came to the town with his wife and scoured the streets for him. On the morning of 20 June he met him near the post office in Wood Street. Kelly accused Stanton of 'knowing' his wife. The traveller admitted that Mrs Kelly had been with him between August 1865 and March 1866 but, said Stanton, he had not at first known that she was married.

As they argued the pair walked down Wood Street and towards the parish church. Kelly demanded that Stanton pay him a hundred guineas as compensation. When Stanton said that he did not have the means to do so, and that they would be better settling their differences via the law, Kelly threatened to murder him.

Meanwhile Mrs Kelly had gone for the police and Constable Wood, Inspector Frost and the Chief Constable, James McDonald, had set out in different directions in search of Kelly and Stanton. It was Wood who came upon them near the

**Figure 23.** *The former police station in King Street in 2001.*

church. Stanton promptly told him that Kelly was threatening his life. Wood suggested they both accompany him to the police station which, in those days, was a small property in King Street. As they went up King Street, Kelly pulled out a gun and fired a number of shots, missing both Stanton and the police officer.

Later the same day, Kelly was brought before the Wakefield magistrates on a charge of attempted murder and was committed for trial at the Assizes. The case was heard in August and, despite a recommendation from the jury for clemency, Kelly was sentenced to ten months' hard labour.

## Chapter 22

# The Poker was not Put Away
# 1871

I f asylum attendant Thomas Lomas had only put the poker away he would not have met so horrible a death.

Lomas, of Newton Lane, was married with a young family. He was a member of the Wakefield Rifle Corps band and was spoken of as possessing tact, bravery and humanity. He had worked at the West Riding Pauper Lunatic Asylum for ten years when, on 24 March 1871, George Lawton, a thirty year old patient, smashed his head and face to a pulp.

Lomas worked on Ward 14, in charge of forty-five patients and with three further staff to assist him. The ward was heated by open coal fires but, except when in use by one of the staff, the poker was kept in a locked cupboard. Lomas had been reminded of the need to lock the poker away only a short time before he was so viciously attacked. Lawton, whose home was

**Figure 24.** *A part of the West Riding Pauper Lunatic Asylum. The clock tower dates from about 1867.*

**Figure 25.** *Some of the wards at the West Riding Pauper Lunatic Asylum.*

**Figure 26.** *The doorway to a padded cell.*
The Stephen Beaumont Museum.

**Figure 27.** *A padded cell.*
The Stephen Beaumont Museum.

at Worsbrough Dale, near Barnsley, had formerly worked as a striker but had been committed to the Asylum on 8 July 1863, He suffered from epilepsy (then, and for many more decades, regarded as a sufficient reason for incarceration) and, although he had attacked a fellow patient at least once, was not generally regarded as in any way dangerous.

On the day of his death, Lomas had remained indoors with Lawton and three other patients whilst the majority of the men had gone out into the garden for fresh air and exercise under the supervision of Benjamin Beaumont and Michael Jordan Killeen. Beaumont heard a cry and, looking up, saw Lawton at a window moving his arm as if striking someone. He rushed back to the ward to find Lomas lying on his back in the padded cell with his face so battered that his brains were spilling out. Lawton was in the day room still holding the poker. With some courage, Beaumont demanded that he hand the poker over but Lawton threatened him, saying, 'If you come near me I will serve you the same'. Beaumont locked the door to the padded cell to protect his colleague from further attack and went to seek help. Whilst he was gone Lawton flung the poker from a window and, upon the arrival of other staff, he was swiftly overcome.

Dr Thompson, the assistant medical officer, went to do what he could for Lomas but he lived for only a few more moments.

It seems that Lomas was in the habit of going to the window of the padded cell to check that all was well with the party of patients in the garden. There had been no friction between Lomas and Lawton but whilst Lomas was looking out, Lawton had come up behind him and struck the first violent blow taking him entirely unawares.

An inquest was held at the Asylum the following day when the foreman of the jury, Mr Coates, a wine and spirit merchant with a business in Kirkgate, inquired how a patient in a lunatic asylum came to have access to a poker. The medical officer, Dr Crichton Browne, admitted that it could only be through the negligence of an attendant. A verdict of wilful murder against Lawton was swiftly pronounced.

Lawton remained at the Asylum during the weekend. It was said that he spent the Sunday gabbling confused prayers for the royal family, his victim, the Wesleyans, the Catholics, and everyone connected with the Asylum. On Monday 27 March he was taken by train, accompanied by his mother and sister as well as by asylum staff, to Leeds where the case was heard at the Assizes. Called to the bar, Lawton seemed unable to answer any questions and Dr Crichton Browne gave his view that he could not understand the meaning of the indictment. The jury promptly decided that he was incapable of pleading and he was sent to Broadmoor.

## Chapter 23

# Murder and Suicide at Eastmoor 1872

I t seems to have been his paramour's alcoholism that led Isaac Townend to strangle fifty-four year old Ruth Hollings in their miserable one-room home in Camplin's Yard, Eastmoor, in July 1872.

Hollings (nee Brooke) was the youngest of a family of nine. She had married Jasper Hollings, a whitesmith, and the couple had lived for a period at the bottom of Westgate, but Hollings had been sentenced to transportation. Quite when Townend, at one time employed with canal boat horses and who was a little younger than his partner, had taken up with Hollings is unclear but the wretched couple had lived together at Eastmoor for a year or so before the murder.

Hollings was described as a quiet and slender man of less than middle height. At the time of the tragedy he was working for John Moxon, a farmer and cab proprietor, driving a horse and cart. He would come home for a meal to find no food in the house and Hollings in a state of intoxication. The room where they lived, in property belonging to Moxon, offered little comfort: it had a few wooden chairs, two deal tables, an ancient clock and a rickety four-post bed. Several of the panes in its two windows were broken and patched up with paper. Hollings' sister, Elizabeth Nichols, lived close by.

On the evening before her death, Hollings had been drinking at the *Fox and Grapes* on Stanley Road and had also been seen, somewhat inebriated, taking some rum to a bed-ridden neighbour in Camplin's Yard.

Isaac Townend had not – it appeared – come to work on the morning of Wednesday 10 July and Moxon's son, William, had been sent to Camplin's Yard to look for him but had gained no answer to his knock. Eventually Moxon went himself. He peered through the window and saw Hollings' body on the

**Figure 28.** *Camplin's Yard where Ruth Hollings and Isaac Townend lived.* The John Goodchild Collection.

**Figure 29.** The Fox and Grapes *where Ruth Hollings was drinking the night before she died.* The John Goodchild Collection.

**Figure 30.** *The* Butchers Arms, *Stanley Road, where the inquest was held into the death of Ruth Hollings.*

bed. He brought in Inspector John Wood of Wakefield Borough Constabulary, who lived in Kitson's Yard. The police surgeon, Dr William Swift Wade, was called at 8.30am and quickly determined that Hollings had been strangled. Townend had been heard to say that he would kill her and then drown himself. No one had any doubt that he was the killer but for a brief time it was assumed that he had then run away.

There was no need to pursue him, however. Later in the morning, Joseph Best, of Caroline Walk, Eastmoor, who was taking a load of manure for Moxon to one of his fields near the waterworks in Ouchthorpe Lane, looked in a shed in the field and saw Townend's body hanging there. He ran to the nearby home of Captain McNeill. As it happened, a West Riding constable, Thomas Edwards, was about to call on him. Edwards went back to the shed with Best. In Townend's pockets he found other evidence of his intention to kill himself - a bottle of poison.

The inquests on both people were held on Thursday, 11 July, that of Hollings at the *Butcher's Arms* in Stanley Road and that of Townend at the *Prince of Wales* inn in Ouchthorpe Lane. The first verdict was of wilful murder, the second of suicide

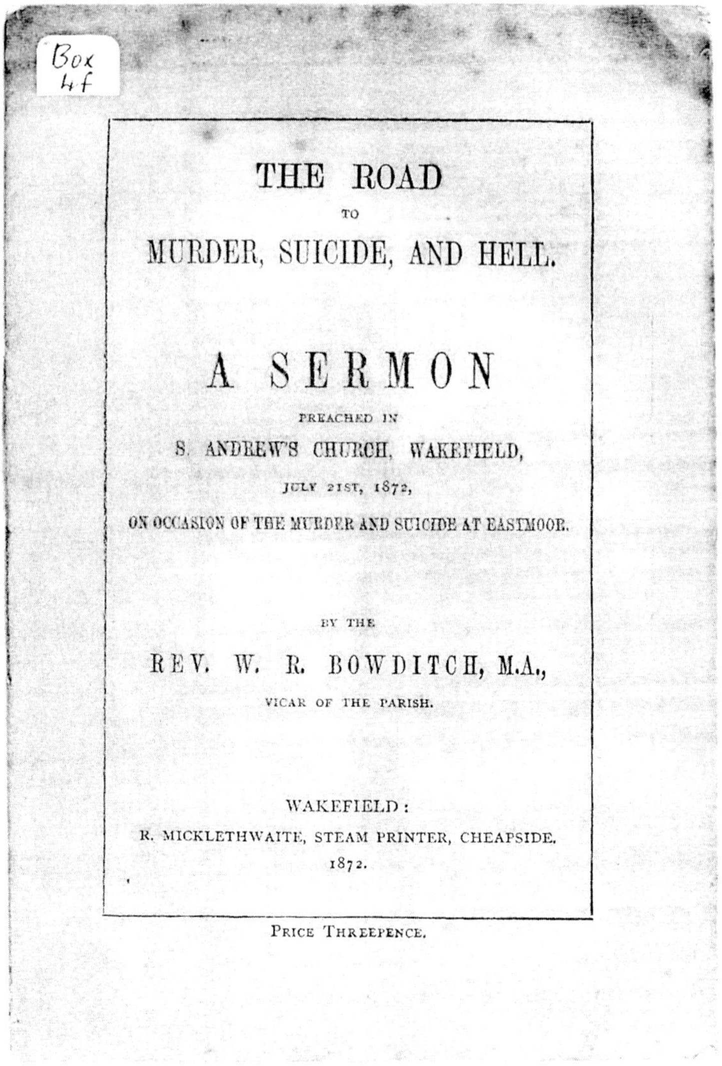

# THE ROAD

TO

## MURDER, SUICIDE, AND HELL.

# A SERMON

PREACHED IN

S. ANDREW'S CHURCH, WAKEFIELD,

JULY 21ST, 1872,

ON OCCASION OF THE MURDER AND SUICIDE AT EASTMOOR.

BY THE

## REV. W. R. BOWDITCH, M.A.,

VICAR OF THE PARISH.

WAKEFIELD:

R. MICKLETHWAITE, STEAM PRINTER, CHEAPSIDE.

1872.

PRICE THREEPENCE.

**Figure 31.** *Title page of the sermon preached by Reverend Andrew Bowditch following the deaths of Ruth Hollings and Isaac Townend.* Wakefield Library Headquarters, Local Studies Collection.

during temporary insanity.

Witnesses at the inquests clearly felt that Townend had been driven to his crime by Hollings' behaviour. But a week later Reverend William Bowditch, vicar of St Andrew's, took the opportunity to preach a sermon on 'the road to murder, suicide and hell'. He claimed that Townend had always been a vicious character.

## Chapter 24

# Was She Beaten to Death?
# 1874

oth Elizabeth Blackburn and Henry Hodgson were widowed when they met and married in the 1874. Elizabeth had two daughters and Henry had a son then only three years old. But Henry was a violent man when angered and Elizabeth was not going to have her children harmed by their stepfather.

In 1876 the family was living in Barratt's Yard, Northgate. Hodgson was a foreman travelling with a steam threshing-machine. His wife, then forty-one, worked on Wednesdays as a waitress at the *Fair House*. Her older daughter, Jane, who was twelve, was employed as a domestic servant by Mrs Walker, the wife of a schoolmaster of College Grove. That summer Elizabeth had consulted the dispensary doctor and she was found to have a weak heart.

On 13 July, Jane was taken ill at work and Mrs Walker sent her home.

Later in the day she went out for a walk with her sister, eleven year old Annie. Elizabeth, who had spent the day toiling over the wash-tub, went out about an hour later to meet them, taking five year old Richard with her. Meanwhile Hodgson had had a little trouble earlier in the day with the police. He had been in Kirkgate and had refused to move on when a police officer told him to do so.

When Elizabeth and her daughters got back to the house, they found Hodgson had come home. He was sitting in his chair, at his ease, with his belt off. He was furious that Jane was not at work. He asked Annie where she had been and hit her with the belt. His wife tried to intervene and Hodgson then struck his wife in the mouth with the buckle. He pursued her into the yard striking her breast with his fist so that she fell, hitting her head against a wall in the yard.

**Figure 32.** *Barratt's Yard, Northgate where the Hodgsons lived.* The John Goodchild Collection.

Jane heard her say, 'You'll have it to pay for'.

Early as the hour still was, the two girls and young Richard went to bed. Shortly afterwards Jane heard her step-father say, 'Lizzie, fetch us a gill of beer' and heard her mother answer, 'You'll have to find the money'. It seems that Hodgson gave his wife a penny and she complied with his request.

Three quarters of an hour later Jane heard a fall. She went downstairs to find her mother lying on her back on the floor but with her knees under her as if she had been kneeling before she fell backwards. There was a group of neighbours round her. She was dead.

Doctor Wade was summoned from York Street and arrived at 7.15pm. He told the inquest jury, at the *Postman Inn* in Northgate, that he found no signs of blood and that externally there were no marks of violence. He confirmed that Elizabeth had heart disease and that she could have died at any time from sudden excitement or a shock. In his view the cause of her death was syncope from heart disease.

The coroner was inclined to terminate the inquest then and there but the jury were far from satisfied and insisted on hearing the evidence of neighbours.

Mary Hartley, also of Barratt's Yard, who was a charwoman and who claimed to have known Elizabeth for twenty-six years, said that she saw Hodgson deliver the blow which caused Elizabeth to fall in the yard. Another neighbour Esther Bodley, whose husband was a shoemaker, had seen Hodgson hit Annie and heard Elizabeth say, 'You sha'n't beat the girl'.

The coroner made every effort to persuade the jury to bring a verdict of natural causes but they were convinced that Hodgson had killed his wife by the blow that caused the fall. The coroner then argued that they must take into account the woman's rebellion in intervening when her husband was beating the girl. Wives, he clearly implied, should accept their husband's rule, and jurors should accept medical evidence.

Again the jury was having none of it and insisted on a verdict of manslaughter against Hodgson. The coroner had no option but to issue a warrant for him to be committed to Wakefield prison to await trial. All three children were taken to the workhouse.

The case was heard in Leeds on 3 August. This time the medical evidence was fully accepted and Hodgson was discharged. But had his harsh treatment really contributed to Elizabeth's death?

## Chapter 25

# A Fight at the Dog Inn 1875

Thomas Carley, a dyer's labourer living in Quebec Street, Wakefield, did his best to stop a fight between Ralph Southern and John Nicholson but he was too late to save Southern's life and to save Nicholson from a charge of manslaughter.

The tragic brawl happened on 7 August 1875. Southern, a healthy, muscular man of forty-four who had been in a relationship for twelve years, was a coalminer. He and his partner, Margaret Smith, lodged with Lucy Spelman and her husband in Quebec Street, Westgate, Wakefield. On that Saturday morning everything seemed normal. Southern had collected his wages and Margaret had met him at the *Coopers Arms* where he handed eighteen shillings (90p) over to her. About five in afternoon the couple went to the *Dog Inn* in Westgate where Southern had two or three glasses of beer. He also helped Carley to move a piano down the stairs. He was in a cheerful mood and sang several songs. About seven o'clock he went to the bar door where he was seen chatting 'in a friendly manner' with John Nicholson and George Wilson, a stonemason's labourer. The three went into the yard and the pub landlady, Martha Turner, saw Nicholson taking off his coat. Anticipating a fight, she called Thomas Carley to go out to them. He found Southern on the ground with Nicholson standing over him, kicking him. He promptly send Nicholson on his way. Wilson later claimed that he was himself too drunk to know anything.

Southern was helped to his feet by Carley and Michael Judge, a puddler at an iron foundry, and went back into the bar where he put his head on the table and said, 'Those two men have killed me.' Nobody, it was said at the inquest, took much notice, but Margaret got him straight home to their lodgings and upstairs to their room. There Southern lay helpless on the carpet and Margaret took off his boots. A local surgeon, William James Lorraine, was called and Southern, who was unconscious, was put to bed. Lorraine ordered a mustard plaster. He returned at intervals throughout the night and during the following day but Southern died on Sunday evening at 8.00pm. The cause of death was a large blood clot resulting from a fractured skull.

Even before Southern had died, Nicholson had been arrested at the house in Westgate where he lodged. He claimed that Southern had been teasing him about a court appearance the previous Wednesday and that this had led to the fight.

The inquest at the *Dog Inn* on Tuesday, 10 August, found

**Figure 33.** *The* Dog Inn *stood on Westgate between Quebec Street and Ings Road, where* PC World *is today.*

that Southern had been 'feloniously killed' by twenty-seven year old John Nicholson. Described as a band spinner at Craddock's rope works, he was brought before the Wakefield magistrates on 11 August and remanded. Two days later George Wilson was also brought before the bench charged with killing Southern. However on 16 August the magistrates decided that no case against Wilson would stand up at the Assizes and he was released. At the same hearing, Nicholson was given bail.

The case against Nicholson was tried at Leeds Assizes on 7 December. In summing up, the judge said that it was clear that Southern had challenged Nicholson to the fight and that the immediate cause of Southern's death was a fracture of the skull caused by his falling. However Nicholson had struck the blow which felled him so that technically he was guilty of manslaughter. The jury confirmed that verdict and the judge sentenced him to one week's imprisonment.

## Chapter 26

# She Could See No Future
# 1875

Twenty-six year old Ellen Coope Carter already had a sixteen-month old toddler, Florence. Unmarried, and now, in 1875, pregnant again, she was afraid of losing her job as a drawer in a worsted mill and could see no hope of a future.

Ellen lived with her younger half-sister, a doubler at the mill, in Ring o'Bells Yard, Horbury. Her step-mother had died seven years earlier. For some years after her mother's death, Ellen had lived with an uncle. There she had had her first child which died when only five weeks old. Seven weeks after her

**Figure 34.** *The river Calder between Durkar and Thornes where Ellen Carter drowned her little girl and herself.*

second child, Florence, was born, Ellen had returned to her work while the little girl was looked after during the day by a series of women including Mary Buttery, Mrs John Goldthorp, and Mrs Sam Steel. Only on Sundays did Ellen have the child herself. Florence's father called at the Ring o'Bells house regularly, albeit very briefly, to leave money for the child's keep.

On Sunday, 22 August, when Ellen was seven months pregnant with her third child, she was manifestly depressed. She wept a good deal and also read from her copy of the New Testament. In the afternoon, taking Florence with her, she called on an old friend, Susannah Shaw, a wool scourer of New Row, Horbury. She asked Susannah to go for a walk with her to California, a wooded area between Horbury Junction and the grounds of Lupset Hall. But Susannah was unwell and mother and child walked away alone.

A little later the pair were seen close to the river Calder by George Senior, a coalminer of Back Lane, Crigglestone. He had been on the other side of the river, sitting on a stile. But he then lay down and saw them no more. He was roused by a scream and, getting up, saw two hats floating in the water. He called to some men in a nearby field and with the help of some boatmen they pulled Ellen from the water at 5.30pm and found Florence at 7.00pm. Both were dead.

The inquest jury found that Ellen had murdered her daughter and then taken her own life whilst temporarily insane.

## Chapter 27

# Child's Peace and Another Noxious Substance, 1875 and 1894

Mr Smith's 'Child's peace' was intended to soothe infants of three months or above but it was a dangerous medicine as John Cullen, a bricklayer living in New Street, and his wife, Ellen, were to discover too late.

In early November 1875 Ellen gave birth to Patrick. She breast fed the baby but also dosed it, newborn though it was, with castor oil. On Sunday, 14 November, when the child was a mere six days old, it seemed to have stomach ache. Ellen had been recommended to try a preparation made up by Westgate druggist, George Smith and referred to as 'Child's Peace'. She bought twopence worth (1p) of the stuff and claimed that the following day she gave Patrick five drops. By the late afternoon the baby was sufficiently ill for John to fetch Doctor William Swift Wade, of York Street. He diagnosed narcotism and asked what Ellen had given the child. She hesitated at first but then admitted to dosing him with Smith's preparation. Little Patrick died just after midnight.

Dr Wade called on the druggist and found that the potion contained opium! The label indicated that it should not be given to children of under three months old but did not mention that it was a poison. No doubt today we would question whether it should be given to any children at all.

At the inquest the verdict was 'accidentally poisoned'.

## 1894

The death of Patrick Cullen was the tragic result of ignorance but the death almost twenty years later of six-week old Benjamin Dews reflected his father's malice. Albert Dews, who was twenty-eight and an ironmoulder, lived with his wife, Eliza, and their two children in Swales Buildings, New

Scarborough, Wakefield. The couple had been married for four years and had a two-year old son, Herbert as well as little Ben. Dews, said to be the black sheep of his family, had a bad reputation. He worked only when he felt like it and spent much of his earnings on drink. He was said to have 'fallen in love' with the girl who became his wife when she was a servant at a public house but he was well known for his cruelty to her, beating and kicking her so that he had twice been brought before the magistrates for assault and on the second occasion had been briefly imprisoned. He had been prosecuted by the National Society for the Prevention of Cruelty to Children for ill-treating little Herbert but the case had been dropped when he claimed that the child's black eyes had been caused by a fall from a chair.

In March 1894, only a few days before Ben was born, Ellen Shannon, who had called at the Dews' house to collect some money that Dews owed to her, witnessed Dews kicking his wife and heard him threaten to kill her. At the same time he swore that the unborn child was not his and that he would not have it in the house.

However once Ben was born a local girl, eleven-year old Eliza Hobson, of Bunkers Hill, Potovens, was employed to assist in the baby's care. On the afternoon of Saturday, 12 May, Dews sent Eliza Hobson to fetch three gills of beer. His wife drank one and he drank the rest himself. He then settled down seemingly to clean a rod. But he was nurturing a terrible scheme. He despatched his wife to buy groceries from Sarah Darling's shop close by. She went, satisfied that Eliza was there watching over the baby. But once his wife had gone, Dews took Benjamin from the servant girl, saying that he would nurse the child himself, and sent her for some more beer. She later said that the child seemed well, strong and comfortable when she left it. When she got back, however, she realized at once that the baby was in agony and, noticing that its breath smelled strange, she asked Dews whether he had given it anything. When the child's mother returned she found the baby on her husband's knee, its mouth was wide open and all the skin gone from around it; its forehead and the side of its face were discoloured and it was vomiting blood. A neighbour, sixteen-

**Figure 35.** The Scarborough Arms, *Alverthorpe Road, where the inquest was held into into the death of baby Benjamin Dews.*

year old Annie Ackroyd, heard the mother screaming and saying, 'Oh, Albert, what have you done to the baby?' She also heard his dreadful response, 'I have done what I said I would do.' Her evidence was later to convict him.

The distraught woman sent Eliza Hobson to fetch Mrs Darling. Dews told his wife to give the baby 'some titty', threatening to cut her breasts off if she did not. But the child could not swallow the milk and continued vomiting blood. Mrs

Darling insisted that they must summon the doctor but Dews stormed that he would not allow him into the house. His wife and Sarah Darling were adamant and Eliza Hobson was sent to fetch Dr Jeremiah Reader. Dews said that the blood must be cleaned up before the doctor came but Sarah Darling told him that the doctor would need to see it. On seeing Ben's state, the doctor was immediately convinced that the child had been given something 'improper'. Suspicion fell at once on Dews and on a bottle of ammonia which Dews had 'borrowed' a little earlier from a workmate who recommended a drop of it to cure toothache but who had warned him that it was poisonous. The bottle had been nearly full; it was now nearly empty. Reader summoned the police and Dews was arrested.

Despite all Reader's attention, Ben died eleven days later after appalling suffering. An inquest was opened the same day at the *Scarborough Arms*. When the jury arrived to view the body, they found a 'sickening sight' as Dr Reader was in the middle of an autopsy. The inquest was adjourned so that the West Riding analyst could examine both the body and the suspect bottle. When it was resumed on 26 May, the jury brought a verdict of wilful murder against Dews.

A special sitting of the magistrates was held inside Wakefield prison on 31 May. He was charged with having 'feloniously and with malice aforethought killed one Benjamin Dews.' Dews, it was reported, seemed little moved although he said, 'It's not right. I have not done anything to the child.' He was committed for trial at the West Riding Assizes.

The trial was held at Leeds on 30 July. Dews' sole line of defence was that he believed the child was not his. He was found guilty of murder but the jury added a recommendation for mercy. The judge was not to be softened and pronounced the sentence of death. Whilst he awaited execution Dews wrote to his wife asking her to do her best 'for poor little Herbert, my son'. Protesting his innocence, he went to the scaffold at Armley Gaol on 21 August.

## Chapter 28

# Pulled off a Water Barrel 1876

When George Knight struck a child with his whip he must have known he was asking for trouble.

The Knights lived in Library Yard, Northgate, Wakefield. Knight was a cart driver employed by Wakefield Corporation and was described as a quiet and inoffensive man. The Scholeys lived nearby in Barratt's Yard. William Scholey was in business as a fruiterer.

On the morning of Monday 24 July 1876 Knight was engaged in watering Northgate (to keep the dust from flying) and had charge of a horse which was pulling the water barrel. One of Scholey's children amused himself by following the barrel and catching the water as it was sprinkled. Ann Page, who kept a shop in Northgate and was married to a colliery engine man named Samuel, saw Knight strike the lad. A few moments later the boy's father came up Northgate and was about to turn into Barratt's Yard when Mrs Page called out to him, 'Whose little boy is that George Knight has hit?'

Within fifteen minutes Knight was making his way back down Northgate to refill his empty barrel with water and was riding on it. Scholey came out of the Yard with his son and asked Knight what he had been doing, repeating several times, 'What's tha say then?' Knight's only response was to urge the horse to 'Gee up'. Upon this Scholey dragged Knight off the barrel. He fell and a wheel of the cart passed over his abdomen. Another witness, Joe Saville, a plasterer, managed to stop the horse.

The first Knight's wife knew of the trouble was when she was called to the then Clayton Hospital in Wood Street where Knight lay unconscious. He died later the same day.

A post-mortem undertaken by Dr Hugh Warriner showed that the wheel had ruptured Knight's liver.

**Figure 36.** *Library Yard, Northgate, where George Knight lived.* The John Goodchild Collection.

**Figure 37.** *The original Clayton Hospital, in Wood Street, where George Knight died.*

An inquest was held the following day at the *Royal Hotel* in Wood Street. The jury's verdict was that Knight had been 'feloniously killed' by Scholey and he was committed to the Wakefield prison with orders given to the Chief Constable, James Aubrough Chipchase, to prosecute him.

On 3 August Scholey came before Leeds Assizes. Questions were raised as to whether Scholey had really pulled Knight off the barrel or whether he had fallen accidentally as he urged the horse forward. However the jury found Scholey guilty. The judge took a lenient view of the case and indicated that his sentence – which he deferred – would be influenced by the level of compensation Scholey was prepared to pay to Knight's widow. Scholey was bound over for the sum of £50 and an uncle made an immediate offer of £30 towards the compensation.

## Chapter 29

# Her Mother was Called a Whore 1876

ose Ann Sweeney was only seventeen when she died on 26 August 1876 after trying to defend her mother's honour.

The Sweeneys lived in Whitehead's Row, off the notorious New Street, Wakefield. Patrick Sweeney was a fishmonger's assistant and whatever else his wife was she certainly enjoyed a drink. Sweeney worked long hours not getting home on Saturdays until 10.30pm or 11.00pm.

On the evening of 12 August a neighbour, thirty-two year old Ann Kilrayne, came to the Sweeneys' door, charged Mrs Sweeney – who was the worse for drink – with being a whore, and knocked her down. William Smith, fettler at a local iron foundry, who lodged with the Sweeneys, pulled Kilrayne away and sent her packing. But Smith and his wife wanted to go out to the market and, fearing more trouble, William woke Rose Ann and asked her to get up to be with her mother in their absence.

Quite how Rose came to be struck by Kilrayne is not clear. The only witnesses to the scene were teenage girls who lived nearby. Emma Marshall, a sixteen-year old spinner in a worsted mill, saw Rose and Kilrayne in the yard where the latter was 'braying' Rose's back with her hands. Amelia Kershaw, who at fourteen was a woollen power-loom weaver, was going to Cooper's shop in New Street about 11.00pm when she heard Rose say, 'Did you want to kill my mother?' and saw her knock at Kilrayne's door with a pair of tongs and then throw a small wash-tub against it. Mrs Kilrayne came out with a poker. A moment later Emma heard Rose say, 'Oh dear, Mother, she has killed me now.'

Hearing cries of 'Murder!' neighbours hurried to the scene, among them Ann Harkin, wife of a bricklayer again named

Patrick. She was later to give evidence of assisting Rose to bed and of Rose asking her to 'Look at my breast where I pulled the poker out'. Ann undressed the girl and had to resort to cutting her stays from her. She went to see Kilrayne who hastened to express regret but who claimed that she had been aggravated.

When Patrick Sweeney returned home Rose was in bed with a group of neighbours standing round her. He heard her say, 'Oh, Father,' two or three times, and then, 'Send for Doctor Wade'.

Wade attended the following morning. He found that Rose had an incision of about half an inch in length in her chest, between the right shoulder and the nipple, which was still bleeding. He attended her regularly but, of course, required payment and the Sweeneys soon succeeded in obtaining the free services of the doctor attached to the charitable Wakefield Dispensary and Clayton Hospital.

From 16 August until her death Rose was attended by Alfred Phillips, the Hospital house surgeon. When he first saw the wound it had scabbed over and seemed to be healing. But the girl was short of breath and coughing. He attributed this to pleurisy.

By Saturday, 26 August Rose was clearly dying. Mary Smith, one of the Sweeneys' lodgers, asked Kilrayne if she wished to see the girl and took her in to Rose's room. She told Rose how sorry she was and, when Rose asked her to pray for her, she knelt by the girl's bed.

Rose died about 10.30pm.

Doctor Wade conducted a post mortem and found that the injury Rose had sustained from the poker had penetrated her right lung which had collapsed. He had, he said at the inquest, noticed black marks round the wound and these could have been made by the poker.

At the inquest, at the *New Market Inn*, the jury brought a verdict of manslaughter against Kilrayne and she was committed to the House of Correction to await charges and trial. She was brought before the Wakefield magistrates on 27 August and remanded for a few days before being committed for trial at the Assizes. At Leeds on 14 December Kilrayne pleaded guilty to the charge of manslaughter. The judge observed, without any irony, that she was someone who bore a character of which any woman ought to be proud. He recognised how remorseful she was and remarked that she had already suffered greatly by being imprisoned. He sentenced her to only a further four days in prison.

The Sweeneys' tragic loss of young Rose Ann had a sad sequel. One of her brothers, Frank, went mad with grief at the death of his sister and was found 'in a wild state' wandering in the street. He was certified insane and committed to the Pauper Lunatic Asylum (later known as Stanley Royd Hospital).

## Chapter 30

# Not Enough Light
# 1876

W hat was Elizabeth Ellen Cardwell doing at Westgate Station, Wakefield, on the evening of 27 October 1876 and why, with a bad foot, did she go out at all? The slipper that she wore over a poultice seems to have caused her death. But there were apparently no witnesses to her fall.

Elizabeth was thirty-four and the wife of James Cardwell, a Wakefield chemist and druggist. She and her husband were lodging with her brother, John Dodds Goldthorpe, a worsted spinner, in Westgate.

Some time between 8.00pm and 9.00pm on the evening in question, Thomas Alderson of Longfield Mount, Alverthorpe, was walking down Westgate when he heard the noise of something falling on the staircase which led up, via three flights of stone stairs, from the street to the 'up' platform. Immediately behind him was William James Lorraine, a surgeon who himself lived in Westgate. The pair went together to investigate. There was a gas light at the foot of the stairs and another one at the top but they found Elizabeth lying on a landing where there was so little light that Lorraine failed at first to recognise her. Alderson went to obtain a lamp from the station and came back with the foreman porter. Elizabeth was lying on her back with her feet towards the bottom of the flight above and with her head in a pool of blood. She was unconscious and Lorraine found a large wound above her left ear. Her slipper was found near the entrance to the steps.

Elizabeth died without gaining consciousness. An inquest was held on 30 October at the *Dog Inn* in Westgate. The jury gave a verdict of accidental death with a recommendation that there should be more lights on the staircase.

Could more light have been shed on the whole episode?

**Figure 38.** *The entrance (now unused) in Westgate to the station, where Elizabeth Cardwell was found part way up the steps.*

## Chapter 31

# The Consequence of Breaking a Colliery Rule, 1877

There was little point in the coroner committing Andrew Hartley for trial on a charge of feloniously killing sixteen-year old Charles Parkin for, on the day after the inquest on Parkin, Hartley himself died. Both deaths were the result of an explosion at Lofthouse Colliery on 18 May 1877. It was Hartley's folly in ignoring a critical colliery rule that led to them..

Andrew Hartley was just twenty-two. He had worked in collieries since he was thirteen and had 'got coal' for some three or four years. He had been at Lofthouse Colliery for only a couple of months when the tragedy occurred. On the day of the explosion he was working 360 yards underground at the coal face in the No. 2 pit. Charles Parkin, of Low Fold, Newton Lane End, was a hurrier working in the same pit. Hartley was in the habit of leaving his lamp at his place while he took his full corf away and coming back with an empty one. He had been warned of the danger of causing an explosion by running his corf into his place if the lamp contained gas.

When Richard Walker, a deputy at the colliery, went on duty at 4.00pm there was, he said, a little gas 'making' in one corner where Hartley worked but he thought there was sufficient air to drive it away without any danger. But when Hartley returned from moving a corf later that day, between 8 and 9pm, he saw a 'blue blaze' in the lamp. The correct procedure, set out in the rules, was for him to pull down the wick to extinguish the lamp by using a 'picker' at its base. Instead he tried to blow it out and, as he said, 'off it went'.

The explosion was heard in No. 1 pit which communicated with No 2. Griffith Hughes and George Scholefield, working in No 1, went to see what had happened. They found Parkin lying beside a full corf. Hughes dragged him for about twenty yards after which he said he would walk. Richard Walker found Hartley sitting in the floor shouting. He took him round the waist and said, 'Come on, lad, let's get out'. Both young men were badly burnt.

The two were put together in a cart to be taken home. Hartley was able to walk into his house with only slight assistance. But Parkin was delirious. His father had him carried upstairs to bed and took off his boots and stockings. His skin came away with them.

Duncan Macarthur, a physician and surgeon attended both lads. Parkin had severe burns on his arms, chest, abdomen and legs; his forehead, temples and back were charred. He died about 3.30am on Sunday, 20 May.

Hartley was still alive when the inquest jury reached its verdict on Parkin on 23 May and the coroner entered in his notes that he was to be committed to the House of Correction (Wakefield prison). But he died at home and an inquest on 25 May brought a verdict in his case of accidentally burnt.

## Chapter 32

# The Baby in the Well
# 1880

**I**n the spring of 1880 the inhabitants of Hawthorn Cottage, a villa in Pinfold Lane, Sandal, began to notice a bad smell. The villa, set in its own grounds and near the site of a former toll bar, was tenanted by a widow, Mrs Ann Westmorland, a woman said to have been 'unfortunate in her servants'. The house had been the property of G H Westerman and was then managed by trustees appointed in his will.

In the middle of June, whilst Mrs Westmorland was conveniently away from home, George Carbutt, the trustees' steward, ordered the drains to be checked, the rainwater cistern to be emptied and plastered, and the well, some twenty-

**Figure 39.** *Hawthorn Cottage, where workmen investigated a bad smell.*

**Figure 40.** *The* Castle Inn, *Sandal where the inquest was held into the remains of the baby's body.*

seven feet deep and six feet in diameter, to be cleaned out. On 21 June, James Brewin, a Sandal bricklayer, went to attend to the cistern whilst Lawrence Ganley and Joseph Siswick pumped the well dry. The work continued into the late evening. When there was a mere eight inches of water left in the well, Carbutt asked Brewin to go down it to check whether any drains emptied into it. With the aid of a ladder and holding a candle, Brewin descended, becoming increasingly aware of a foul stench as he went down.

To his horror, as he neared the bottom Brewin saw the feet and head of a child. Siswick went to find Constable Hodgson whilst Brewin went to summon Carbutt. Then, by putting a piece of sacking under it, Ganley and Brewin brought the body up. Siswick apparently could not face the task and Ganley said afterwards that the body had 'burst' and that he would rather walk twenty miles than perform such a task again. It entirely put him off his food.

The remains were placed in a wheelbarrow and taken to an outhouse at the *Castle Inn* and a telegram was send summoning Mrs Westmorland in case she should be needed at the inquest. Doctor John Whiteley, of Southgate, examined the corpse. He told the inquest, which was held at the *Castle Inn* the next day, that the body had probably been in the water for four or five months. It was much decomposed and nothing remained of the lungs so that it was quite impossible to say whether it had ever lived or had been stillborn.

The jury reached a verdict that the baby had been found in a well but that there was insufficient evidence to show whether it had ever lived. The Coroner observed that the only action the police might take would be to bring a charge of concealing a birth. Suspicion, according to the *Wakefield Express* fell on a 'former domestic' in Mrs Westmorland's employment.

## Chapter 33

# The Unfaithful Wife
# 1880

No one, it seems, had a hard word to say for Thomas Beckett when he killed his wife, twenty-nine year old Hannah, on 15 December 1880.

Thomas and Hannah had been married for more than ten years. Hannah, whose maiden name was Marshall, came from a farming family at Whitton Run in Norfolk and in the late 1860s had been in service at the farm of Mr Balgue of Crofton where she had met Thomas. After their marriage, in Crofton Church, Thomas had obtained employment with a Walton farmer who provided a cottage for the couple. But some 'misunderstanding' had occurred and Thomas had left, finding work at Hemsworth Fitzwilliam Colliery and moving with his wife to a hovel in Old Soaphouse Yard, close to the Barnsley Canal in Walton.

Here there were eight single-storey cottages, each with just two rooms and described at the time of Hannah's death as 'more suitable for stables than for human habitation'. The back room was the Becketts' bedroom and the front room doubled as kitchen and parlour and had a 'shut-up' bed where the Becketts' lodger, Hannah's brother, Robert Marshall, slept. Robert was a canal labourer.

Thomas normally got up at five in the morning and walked the five miles to his work at the pit, usually in the company of a fellow miner, Thomas Walden. He would return home, again on foot, about 5.00pm. He was said to be a quiet man and a teetotaller. He gave the whole of his wages, some 27s 3d [£1.37p] a week, to his wife.

But Hannah, according to reports in the *Wakefield Express* was a bad lot. And certainly she had, in the months before her death, taken up with a lover. This was one Harry Ogden of Newmillerdam, whose own wife had left him for a married man and gone off to America. Some weeks before her death, Hannah had lived with Ogden for a week or more but had returned to Beckett who, it was said, had taken her back without reproach. On 11 December, just four days before her death, Hannah had spent the day in Wakefield in Harry's company and had gone back to Newmillerdam with him for the night although she had gone home again the following day.

But Thomas had had enough, as he confided to his workmate, Thomas Walden. On 15 December he arrived home from work to meet Hannah, all dressed up, as she was coming out of the Yard. She told him she was going into Wakefield to see Hamilton's Diorama at the Corn Exchange. Thomas asked whether she expected to meet Harry and she brazenly confirmed that she did. Thomas ordered her home and, once inside the cottage, told her he could stand no more of it and it would be best if he killed himself. Somehow – and swiftly – the couple made a pact. Each would kill the other. Elizabeth seized a knife and Thomas took up the razor which both he and his brother-in-law used.

Only a few moments later Robert Marshall too came home from work. But, as he found the door locked and there was no answer to his knock, he went to the lodging house near the canal bridge for half an hour or so to spend time with his mates. There was still no reply when he returned to the cottage so he went round to the back where paper had been put up in place of missing window-glass. He stepped into the Becketts' bedroom. There he found the couple, both lying fully dressed on top of the bed-clothes, Thomas with one arm underneath Hannah and the other across her breast. Hannah was clearly dead and Thomas fast bleeding to death.

Marshall fetched Constable Newton who sent for Doctor John Whiteley, the West Riding Police surgeon. Whiteley pronounced Hannah dead and dressed Thomas's wounds. He was moved into the front room to occupy the shut-up bed, watched over by two police officers, and Hannah was left on the marriage bed.

There Hannah remained until Saturday, 18 December when she was buried in a pauper's grave in a remote corner of Sandal churchyard. The sole mourner was her brother.

**Figure 41.** *The soaphouse yard area has been redeveloped but a building associated with Hodgson and Simpson's soapworks can still be seen in the background of this picture.*

The inquest on Hannah, on 17 December, found that she was murdered by Thomas Beckett and the coroner issued a warrant for him to be moved to the prison in Wakefield. By 19 December he had recovered sufficiently for the move to take place and he was taken to the prison hospital.

Thomas was tried on the charge of murder at the Assizes in

Leeds on 5 February 1881. A Walton farmer, S Bailey Walker, had been immensely busy about his defence and, not only providing the finances for it, he also gave evidence on the prisoner's behalf. Thomas was treated with remarkable gentleness and was offered a chair rather than being expected to stand in the dock. Much was made of Hannah's wickedness and Thomas's forbearance. The prosecuting barrister told the jury that if they thought they could 'best discharge their duty' by bringing in a verdict other than the one he felt bound to ask for (ie guilty of murder), the verdict would be one 'which the prosecution would recognise'.

The defending barrister brought tears to the eyes of many of the onlookers. He told the jury that they had, of course, a duty to the public but that they also had a duty to the 'unhappy man' in the dock. The judge carefully explained the difference between murder and manslaughter. If the jury thought that Thomas had had 'recent and grave provocation' before he killed Hannah, and might have been regarded as 'not being master of his reason', then the case was simply one of manslaughter.

It took the jury a mere fifteen minutes to agree on the lesser verdict.

The judge said that he concurred with that verdict and pronounced sentence of four days' imprisonment which meant, since Thomas had served rather more than that, that Thomas could be freed immediately.

Thomas had been expecting a sentence of up to seven years' hard labour and, being somewhat deaf, he thought the judge had imposed a fourteen-year sentence. However the misapprehension was soon corrected and his solicitor took him to the railway station and put him on a train for Huddersfield where his father and other members of his family lived.

## Chapter 34

# The Faked Suicide Note
# 1884

**I**n the terms of our own day, Richard Lee Dugdale would have been seen as 'upwardly mobile'. Born illegitimate, he had begun life as a spinner in a textile mill in his home town of Burnley. There, too, he worked as a railway porter, but, after marrying a local girl by the name of Smith, he had moved to Barnsley to become chief clerk in the goods office of the Manchester, Sheffield and Lincolnshire Railway Company. He changed jobs again to work for Paul

**Figure 42.** *Wesley Street where the 'upwardly mobile' Richard Lee Dugdale lived.*

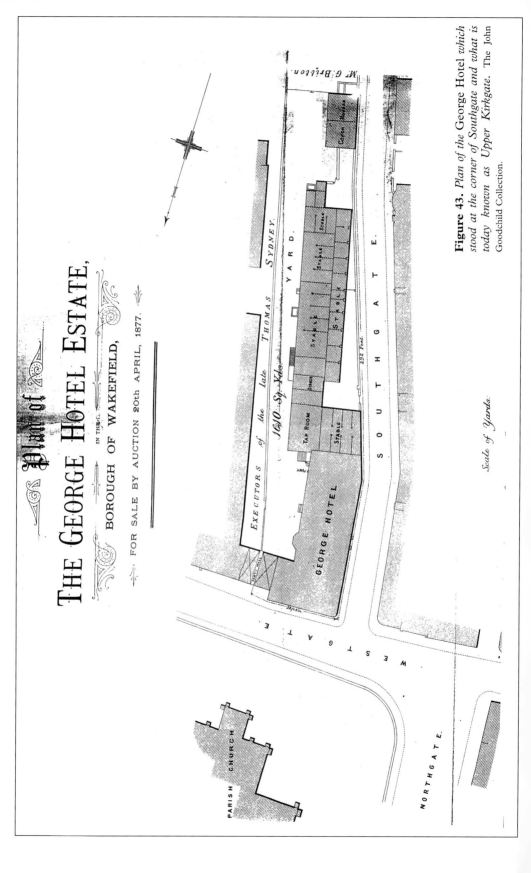

and Guy Senior before becoming a commercial traveller for a Mr Locke, Maltster, of Hoyle Mill, Barnsley. At the time of his murder in 1884 he was thirty-seven and was travelling on behalf of John Austin of Red Hill House, Castleford, whose family firm, Austin Brothers, had maltings in Allerton Bywater, Castleford, Kippax and Wakefield. He was living at 3 Wesley Sreet, Belle Vue, Wakefield, and had six children aged between ten months and thirteen. He was spoken of as a respectable man who was an active member of Court 1622 of the Ancient Order of Foresters and was active, too, in the Hospital Sunday movement.

Whether Dugdale was altogether such a pillar of society might be questioned and it could certainly be argued that his own lack of judgment, of not, indeed, his folly, led to his quite horrible death.

In the week of 29 September Dugdale was due to call on some of his firm's customers in Lancashire but he was engaged in Wakefield on the Tuesday of that week and did not set out until the Wednesday. This meant that on Friday, instead of being able to return to Wakefield and attend the corn market as he should have done, he had to spent a further night – the night of his death – in Bolton. Meanwhile he had sent the orders he had collected by telegram to the Austins.

But what was he doing in Wakefield on 30 September? The episode is not an edifying one! He was appearing in the County Court to sue William Fielding, proprietor of the *George Hotel* (which stood on the corner of Upper Kirkgate and Southgate) for the return of £1. And, moreover, though he was soon 'rumbled' by Fielding's solicitor, he was acting under the name of Richard Lee, having omitted the surname of Dugdale. He had, he claimed, been in the *George* when a dispute arose as to whether the local soap-manufacturing firm was named Hodgson and Simpson or Hodgson and Simpsons. He had gone for the latter, others were sure (and they were right) that Simpson had no final s. Another member of the group, Jo Woodhead, had bet Dugdale £1 that the name was Simpson. Dugdale had taken the bet and each had placed a £1 coin on a tray whilst Fielding looked for the evidence of a bill-head in his files. Dugdale seems to have regretted his rashness for he claimed that he told the company that it was a silly thing to make the subject of a wager and that anyway betting was illegal and he proposed taking his £1 back. Fielding, however, confirmed the true name of the firm and handed both sovereigns to Woodhead. And, of course, in 1884 £1 was a not inconsiderable sum of money.

So perhaps when he went on to Lancashire to pursue his occupation, Dugdale needed to re-establish his self esteem.

Dugdale's work seems to have consisted of progressing from one public house to another, taking orders for malt and collecting payments and, incidentally, enjoying a few drinks. On the day he met his death he was to be found by half-past ten in the morning in the *Fleece* in Bolton where he had a drink or two with a friend of some years, one Robert Hall, an oil merchant. They were joined by 25-year old Kay Haworth (or Howarth), a stranger to Dugdale but a young man whom Hall seemed to know well. Haworth, a native of Egerton and described as a borer by trade, had only recently returned from America. He was living in lodgings in Bolton but was without employment and apparently dependent on the goodwill of an uncle living locally at whose house he took most of his meals. Perhaps he was something of a professional sponger. Certainly he seems to have been of a merry disposition and not averse to being a convivial drinking partner if others stood each round. Dugdale was evidently happy to stand treat. He was also happy to flash his money – or his employer's money – around, showing off a cheque for £3 that one Entwistle had given him which led Hall to remark that it would be easy to alter the figure on the cheque to £30. From the *Fleece* the trio went on to the *Hare and Hounds*, the *One Horse Shoe* and other public houses before going for 'dinner' at a restaurant close to the *Fleece*. By the time they had all visited the *Fleece* again, Dugdale was feeling sick and was much the worse for drink and at the *Crown and Cushion* the landlord refused to serve them. Dugdale decided to return to his lodging at the *Wheatsheaf* and it was left to Haworth to undertake to take him there.

Oddly Haworth rejoined Hall quite shortly and announced that Dugdale had refused to go to the *Wheatsheaf* and he had left him at Mawdsley Street Chapel close to the *Balmoral* hotel. Haworth then went on to the theatre where a fellow lodger noticed how swollen his hands were and Haworth explained that he had had a dispute with someone over a game of dominoes and had beaten him up. After the performance he had gone on to the *Three Crowns*, buying brandies for himself and treating other customers with considerable liberality. He showed the barmaid a fistful of money and invited her to go to the United States with him.

But at 9.15pm the same evening a farrier, William Quinn, who lived in Silverwell Lane, went out to dump some bottles on waste land behind a furniture warehouse in nearby Claire Street. Seeing a rather suspicious object, he fetched a neighbour and a lamp. The object was Dugdale, lying in a little hollow, with his coat and vest unbuttoned, his arms raised above his head and an old pocket knife lying loosely in his right hand. His eyes were cut and swollen, his face was smeared with blood and his throat was slit. He was quite dead. Quinn fetched the police and Dugdale was taken to the mortuary.

Very little money beyond some coppers and a threepenny bit was found on the body but there was a pocket book, in which Dugdale's business transactions were neatly recorded, but in which, also, were scrawled the words, 'done through one sede (sic) of mind, goodbye all', evidently intended to pass as a – remarkably illiterate – suicide note.

Haworth came under suspicion immediately. The police called at his lodgings where they found him still in possession of £32 in gold, a further 18s in silver, a watch, bills and other documents which had been in Dugdale's possession. His coat sleeve, vest, trousers and shoes were smeared with blood. Moreover witnesses had seen him walking arm-in-arm with Dugdale along Silverwell Street, in quite the opposite direction to either the *Balmoral* or the *Wheatsheaf*.

An inquest was held on 6 October in Bolton Town Hall. A verdict of wilful murder was brought against Haworth who was committed to Strangeways Prison to await trial at Manchester Assizes. He was tried on 4 November, found guilty of murder and sentenced to death. He was executed ten days later.

## Chapter 35

# Eight Months on the Run 1887

W ould David Pilmore have ever been apprehended if he had not given himself up, in Reading, after making rather too merry on Christmas Day? And had he intended to kill his victim or was the shooting, near Badsworth, an accident?

Born in Sheffield in June 1863, the son of a police officer, Pilmore was a bright lad and, coming from a respectable family, a diligent attender at Sunday School. He went to day school first at Brampton, then to Caseley's School, Wath-on-Dearne, where he attended a chapel built by the owner of the local oil works, and finally to school in Kilnhurst. He was then apprenticed to a stone mason. But for David respectability was, perhaps, no more than a veneer. Certainly the newspaper reports of the shooting painted a very black picture of him. In his teens he became an expert poacher; he was arrested at Swinton and – not surprisingly considering his father's employment – he was found to have a careful, and obviously useful, record of the local police officers' beats on him. When an explosion was caused by a canister of gunpowder being flung into a house in Wath during a miners' strike, Pilmore was said to have been a prime suspect.

After three-and-a-half years, Pilmore left the mason and went to work in the coal mines where the pay was higher. By the time he shot and killed Edward George Copley, he was living in lodgings near Cudworth and was employed at Monk Bretton; he had already worked in collieries at Barnsley, Rotherham and Mexborough. He was twenty-four.

Copley was an under-keeper, or game-watcher, on Captain Richard Heywood Jones's Badsworth Hall estate. He was at work shortly after daybreak on 29 April 1887 with the head keeper, William Illingworth, close to Elmsall Lodge, when the

**Figure 44.** *The house tenanted by George Nicholson to which William Illingworth went for help.*

pair saw two men on the footpath from South Kirkby behaving in a way that aroused their suspicions. Illingworth followed them, sending Copley round by J Honley's farm to get ahead of them and intercept them. Illingworth was a very experienced gamekeeper who had worked for the Grove Hall estate for some twenty years before entering Jones's service in 1882. He approached the men and advised them that they must find better ways of spending their time. Pilmore and his companion, Harry Roberts, made it plain that they resented being followed but Illingworth continued to trail them. He 'got into a willow garth', he was later to say, from which he saw one of the poachers shoot into a field. Pilmore then went into the field himself whilst, according to Illingworth, Roberts remained on the roadway and re-loaded the gun. Illingworth then continued to follow the pair as they walked in the direction of Badsworth old toll bar. Near the bar – again according to Illingworth, the younger poacher took the gun from his companion and aimed it at the gamekeeper but without firing a shot. The two poachers then went onto the railway line and headed towards South Kirkby, Illingworth still following them. But they saw Copley ahead of them and turned instead for Hemsworth. The older poacher, Roberts, it was said at Pilmore's trial, threw a stone at Illingworth who retaliated in like manner. Pilmore, holding the gun then in his left hand, also threw a stone, or stones, at Illingworth. Roberts then ran at Illingworth with a stake. As the gamekeeper began to get the better of his assailant, Pilmore was alleged to have said that he would 'blow a hole through' Illingworth, and to have raised the gun to his shoulder. Copley came running up and, in the ensuing affray, Pilmore, shot him from close range. He fell to the ground. Roberts and Illingworth continued to struggle and Roberts too fell, dragging Illingworth down with him. Pilmore then hit Illingworth with the butt of his gun.

The fracas took place on farmland tenanted by George Nicholson, in a field sown with spring wheat. Despite his own injuries, Illingworth ran to the farm, variously known then as Badsworth Grange and Badsworth Common, for assistance. Nicholson provided a conveyance and Copley was taken home. Meanwhile someone had gone for Dr Wood, of Ackworth, who went immediately – about 6.00am – to attend to the injured game-watcher. Wood was .gravely concerned at the extent of the injury, a wound some three-and-a-half inches wide in his chest. Copley's shirt and waistcoat had to be drawn out of the hole which also contained sixty-eight shotgun pellets. Wood summoned a colleague, Dr Buncle, of Purston, meanwhile remaining himself for two hours applying pressure to Copley's chest in an effort to stop the flow of blood. But, although both Wood and Buncle returned to attend Copley several times in the next few hours, there was little that they could do for him.

Copley remained conscious almost to the end. A local magistrate, Colonel W J F Ramsden of Rogerthorpe Manor, came to obtain his deposition, given 'in expectation of approaching death', which was taken down, in the Colonel's presence, by Philip R Christie of the firm of Leatham, Pontefract who was later to practise as a solicitor in Brighton. Shortly before he died, Copley asked to see Illingworth. The two shook hands. Copley asked the gamekeeper to move him a little and he died in his arms. It was the afternoon of 30 April, the day following the shooting.

Meanwhile the police were hunting for the two poachers. Neither could be found but a gun was retrieved from Harry Roberts' home. Its barrel was dirty, with burnt powder on it as if it had been recently discharged.

On the day after Copley's death, Sunday, 1 May, the Master of Hemsworth Grammar School, Reverend E S Butler, conducted the service at Badsworth Church, taking the opportunity to preach about the tragedy. A reporter spoke of 'tears and sobs rising from the bosoms of strong manhood'.

An inquest was held on Monday, 2 May in the Reading Room, near to the church, at Badsworth before Dr Grabham, the coroner. William Illingworth, who had injuries to his head and over his right eye, was able to attend and give evidence. He identified the gun as the one that had been used to shoot Copley. The dead man's statement was read. The verdict was one of wilful murder against David Pilmore and Henry Roberts.

Copley was buried the same afternoon, in Badsworth churchyard. The funeral was attended by Copley's employer, Captain Jones, and several other local gentlemen, including Colonel Ramsden. It was conducted by the curate of Hemsworth, Reverend T Husband. Copley left a wife and two children. He also had two sisters in Pontefract, one a Mrs Firth and the other a teacher at the National girls' school. A gravestone was erected in memory of Copley at the expense of Captain Jones and his daughter.

**Figure 45.** *The Reading Room, Badsworth, where the inquest on Edward George Copley was held.*

Pilmore and Roberts made good their escape. Descriptions of both men were widely circulated. Pilmore was said to be about 5ft 11ins in height, with a thin face, brown eyes, a sallow complexion and prominent cheek bones. He was thought to be wearing a blue pilot jacket, dark cord vest and trousers, a black billycock hat, stong laced-up boots and a grey-blue peaked cap. But the pair were not to be found. They hid in woodlands by day and walked by night. Quite where – and in what circumstances – the pair separated is something of a mystery. Pilmore went from London to Windsor and then on to Reading where, under the name of Charles Wilman, he enlisted with the B Company of the Berkshire Regiment. Here, at Christmas, he told Corporal Thomas Henry Webb about the affray at Badsworth whilst insisting that he had never intended to kill Copley.

Pilmore was brought back to Yorkshire and came before Pontefract magistrates on 31 December. He was remanded and taken to the prison in Wakefield. He came before the magistrates again on 11 January and was committed for trial at the West Riding Assizes in Leeds. The case was heard on 21 February 1888. Pilmore was described as standing in the dock in a 'bold, soldierly manner' and he pleaded not guilty to the charge of murder. Police Constable Frank Robinson gave evidence of having seen Pilmore and Roberts together at Houghton Common on the day before the shooting. He had noticed something bulky in Pilmore's pocket and Pilmore had showed him a gun, producing a licence for it. Illingworth, who was, of course, the only living witness to the events of 29 April, gave his version of the encounter with the poachers and the subsequent shot, and the deposition made by Copley before his death was read to the court.

Copley appeared to have agreed to the words 'I struck at the gun and missed it'. However the words and missed it had been crossed out and the correction had been initialled by Colonel Ramsden. Remarkably the Colonel could not, at the trial, remember why this was but Pilmore's defending counsel urged that it was because Copley had never said them. Rather, it was Copley's knocking the gun that caused it to go off: Pilmore had never intended to fire a shot at all.

In his summing up the judge advised the jury that premeditation was not fundamental to a charge of murder. It was enough that Pilmore intended to shoot Copley at the time. Pilmore was swftly found guilty. When the judge asked him why sentence of death should not be passed, he said, quietly and respectfully, 'Speech is useless now, Sir.' He was taken to the condemned cell with orders that a watch be kept on him night and day until his execution.

However, there were those who were far from satisfied by Pilmore's trial. Foremost among these was Joseph Parker Howe, a lawyer who found flaws amounting to what he regarded as a 'flagrant' case of injustice: the judge had admitted a critical statement that was clearly false and had summed up quite unfairly; Pilmore should not have been convicted of the capital charge of murder and should perhaps not have been convicted at all.

Howe argued that the gamekeepers had far exceeded their powers in pursuing Pilmore and Roberts and that Pilmore was right to defend himself against unlawful arrest. All that the gamekeepers were empowered to do in law was to ask the poachers for their names and addresses. If the poachers refused to give them, then the gamekeepers might arrest them. But neither Illingworth nor Copley had sought their names. Then Pilmore had told his father that he did not know that the gun was loaded: he had shot at the hare and gone into the field to see if he had hit it, and it was whilst he was doing that, unknown to him at the time, Roberts had re-loaded it. He had not intended to shoot but Copley had caught his arm and the gun had gone off accidentally. Moreover it was Illingworth who had thrown the first stone, not Roberts. Roberts had been seriously injured by Illingworth and had a deep wound at the back of his head. Copley had told the policeman who arrested him in Reading that Roberts had died from the injury. The men had never armed themselves to resist gamekeepers but simply to bag a few hares.

Much had depended on the statement given by Copley as he lay dying that he 'struck at the gun and missed it'. Howe insisted that it was quite wrong of the judge to allow the words 'and missed it' to stand in evidence.

Howe had expected questions to be raised about the verdict after the trial but, as nothing was apparently being done, he wrote himself to the Home Secretary and to the *Yorkshire Post* setting out his concerns. He succeeded in rousing public opinion and in prompting Pilmore's solicitor and his defending counsel to prepare a petition on Pilmore's behalf. Articles appeared in other newspapers, the *Manchester Courier*, for example, arguing that Pilmore should not be executed as he had never intended to kill Copley. In Leeds in the space of a few days almost 40,000 signatures were collected on the copies of the petition distributed at such places as the Holbeck Liberal Club, the offices of the *Leeds Mercury*, and the *Waverley Hotel*. In Barnsley a forty-foot long petition carried some 4,000 names.

The pleas for clemency were successful and, as the scaffold was being prepared, the Home Secretary commuted the sentence to one of life imprisonment.

## Chapter 36

# The Murder Weapon was a Kneeling Board, 1889

**E**very moment of our lives we run the most fearful risks, claimed Dr William Bevan Lewis, medical superintendent at the West Riding Pauper Lunatic Asylum, after one of his patients, Robert Hurst, had smashed the skull of another patient, forty-seven year old William Latham.

The murder occurred on the morning of Sunday, 2 June 1889. Hurst and Latham were both held in Ward 1, or the Refractory Ward, which was for the most difficult male patients. Latham had come from Goole where he had been a farm labourer. He suffered from chronic melancholia and before his admission had twice attempted to drown himself. But he was said also to be quarrelsome and discontented and to upset other patients by interfering with their work. Six weeks before his death he had tried to strangle another patient.

Hurst had been a soldier, serving for seven years in the York and Lancaster Regiment before being discharged as suffering from sunstroke. He had been in Netley Hospital before coming to the asylum, which was close to his family home at Primrose Hill, on 20 June 1884. He was said to suffer from 'the very

**Figure 46.** *A scale model made by Mr L Ashworth, of the original H-block at the West Riding Pauper Lunatic Asylum.* Wakefield District Heritage.

worst delusional insanity' with 'aural hallucinations' and 'delusions of persecution by unseen agents'. He had appeared to believe that he was in a coffin awaiting burial whilst feeling bullets passing through him. Perhaps there was a strain of insanity in the family – he had an aunt in the asylum and another aunt had died there – or perhaps his experiences in fighting had unhinged his mind. He was also regarded as one of the most violent men in the institution and had in the past attacked a charge attendant and threatened others.

On Sundays the patients rose at seven o'clock (on weekdays they got up at six). Hurst and Latham went to the ward scullery to gather equipment needed for their task of cleaning some of the rooms. Two of the attendants, Joe Ibbeson and William Henry Wallace, heard a scuffle and found Hurst standing with a kneeling board in his hand and Latham lying unconscious on the floor. He had extensive fractures to the skull. Dr Lewis and Dr Buller operated to remove fragments of bone but Latham died the same day. A post mortem found a large bloodclot in the skull. Dr Lewis gave his opinion that death was the result of shock and that the kneeling board could have caused the injuries he found. The board, made of wood was an inch thick, measured some eighteen by nine inches and weighed four-and-three quarter pounds.

The foreman of the inquest jury, an Eastmoor blacksmith named Faux, was very concerned that violent and unmanageable patients should have access to items – such as buckets and kneeling mats – that they could use to inflict injury. But Lewis insisted that they needed some form of work and that, although they had had kneeling boards for fifteen years, this was the first problem they had had. Prior to purchasing these, the inmates who scrubbed floors had been given knee pads but these had soon been torn up.

Again the jury were critical of the level of supervision of such violent patients but Dr Lewis argued that he would need an enormous increase of staff to provide a ratio of more than one member of staff to eight such patients and that he had a hundred or more who were as difficult as Hurst.

The jury's verdict was that Latham had been murdered by Robert Hurst and he was committed for trial at Leeds Assizes.

## Chapter 37

# A Fight at the Harewood Arms 1889

There was always considerable doubt as to whether George Brown had really been responsible for the death of twenty-four year old Jack Cullen, a bachelor miner lodging in New Street and employed at Park Hills Colliery. What was clear, however, was that the two had been involved in a fight at the *Harewood Arms* in Kirkgate during the early evening of Saturday 7 December 1889 and two days later Cullen was dead.

Cullen's father, John Cullen, was a carter and lived close to his son in New Street. That Saturday morning the pair had been busy moving furniture for a Mr Garbert from Hope Street to Albion Street. They had finished about three o'clock and had gone together for a drink at the *New Elephant* public house, in New Street, before Jack left to go into town. Later Cullen was with a group of young men in the *Harewood Arms* and had become considerably the worse for drink. He and Brown had begun to quarrel and then to fight and the landlord, James William Eastwood, had turned them out into the back yard. There two other labourers, George Mathery and Henry Hobson, both of Avison's Yard, found them with Brown on top of Cullen, striking him. Hobson took Brown's arm and Mathery told him, 'That will do'. A further labourer, Walter Boyle, who lived at South Street, Primrose Hill, took Cullen to the bottom of Warrengate and washed his face in the springs at the Wavers. The pair then went for a beer to *No 6*, in the Springs, but Cullen could drink only a little. He complained that his head ached and he wanted only to get home.

Before going to his own lodging, at Sarah Clift's, Cullen had dropped in on his father. His face was bruised and swollen but he made no complaint. The following day father and son went together again to the *New Elephant* but that evening Cullen was

**Figure 47.** *The* Harewood Arms, *Kirkgate, in 2001.*

dizzy and began to vomit blood. He had gone to sleep but was rambling. The next morning he was found unconscious. John Cullen made all the effort he could to obtain medical assistance. He tried first to get Dr Haley to attend his son. He then went for Dr Wade but found he had gone to the Assizes in Leeds. He tried Dr Statter but was told that he was at dinner. Finally in the early evening he fetched Dr Roulstone but was greeted before they reached Mrs Clift's with the news that his son was dead. But Dr Haley's assistant, Mr Wainman, had been to look at Jack at one o'clock and had ordered that brandy cloths be applied to his head. He was sufficiently alarmed to return at three o'clock with Inspector Wright. The latter had then gone with Constable Illingworth to arrest Brown on a charge of unlawful beating.

The inquest was held the next day, Tuesday 10 December, at the *New Elephant*, before Thomas Taylor. Brown wept as he heard the evidence. Haley and Wainman described the results of their post-mortem examination. They had found external bruising to the face but no internal injuries to the brain and no inflammation. Cullen's heart was healthy although his lungs were slightly congested. They believed that if he had stayed in bed and rested throughout Sunday he would still have been alive. Death was due, however, in their view, to concussion. Mr Lodge, representing Brown, suggested that this might have resulted from a fall rather than the fight. The inquest was adjourned for a day to allow for a further post-mortem, this time by Dr Wade.

It resumed on Wednesday, 11 December at the City Police Office. Dr Wade, too, could find no internal injury although he noted that the brain was somewhat drained of blood; this had, he said, caused syncope.

Five of the jury were quite ready to regard this as an accidental death although seven believed Brown to be guilty. For a time, despite a number of visits to their room by the coroner, it seemed that they would never reach agreement. But in the end the minority gave way and a verdict of death by a blow from George Brown was pronounced. Brown, the father of three, who lived at 49 Roberts and Smiths Buildings, Eastmoor, was granted bail.

Brown had next to appear before the magistrates. The hearing took place a week later, on 18 December. There was little new evidence except that Brown's father insisted that Cullen had struck the first blow and had held Brown down over him by holding tightly to his neck-handkerchief so that Brown had had to strike him to obtain his release. Brown was committed for trial at the Assizes but was again given bail.

Brown had to wait until 18 March 1890 to know his fate. But the evidence at Leeds Assizes was in his favour. The jury was told that it was Cullen who had started the fight and that he had never subsequently laid any complaint against Brown. Dr Wade gave his view that if Cullen had had proper attention from the first he would not have died. Brown left the court a free man.

## Chapter 38

# The Jealous Husband
# 1890

Jealousy in a young husband, whilst regrettable, is entirely understandable, but it is much harder to accept the jealousy that led sixty-seven year old William Whittlestone to beat his sixty-four year old simple-minded wife to death.

The Whittlestones lived at Durkar – or Dirtcar as it was then known – close to the *New Inn* in a cottage with a modest garden. William worked as a road labourer. Sarah was said to be 'decent and hardworking' but 'childish or idiotic' She had, apparently, by the time of her death, little idea of doing housework or of getting William's meals on time. It seems, too, that she liked to smoke and that she would accost men as they passed the cottage to beg tobacco off them. William was given to fits of jealousy and frequently assaulted poor Sarah.

It was on the afternoon of Monday, 17 March 1890 that William, returning home from work at about 5.30pm, set about his wife for the final, fatal time. He accused her of sitting in the cottage with the door open especially to watch out for 'Tom' with whom, he alleged, she had been intimate. She denied this and he felled her to the ground with a piece of garden rail, continuing to belabour and kick her.

The door remained open and a neighbour, Samuel Linnington, or Rimmington, saw William standing over his wife as she lay on the floor. He was afraid of being late for the night shift at Marsden's paper works at Calder Grove and hurried on, but he heard blows as he went.

Children gathered round the door to watch the fearful spectacle. Frederick Lane, a young pit hurrier on his way home from Horbury stopped to see what they were looking at and saw William kicking Sarah. William then turned on Lane, threatening him with a garden fork.

**Figure 48.** The New Inn, *Durkar, where the inquest into the death of Sarah Whittlestone was held.*

After beating Sarah for an estimated thirty minutes, William ordered her to get his tea ready and went into the garden to plant some beans. Ellen Clarkson, another neighbour, saw Sarah come into the garden herself to empty some tea leaves and noticed how dreadful her face looked and how weak she seemed. She suggested to her brother that they should inform the police and he and another man reported their anxiety to Constable Little. Little called round at the Whittlestones' cottage about 9.00pm, but finding the door locked and obtaining no answer, he left. However he reported the matter to a superior officer, Sergeant Robert Chalkley.

The following afternoon Chalkley went himself to the cottage and found Sarah in a critically-injured state. He ordered William to go to fetch the doctor. William did so, telling the doctor that he had thrashed his wife for committing adultery. The doctor went directly to Whittlestone's cottage and examined Sarah finding her face badly cut and bruised and extensive bruises on her legs and abdomen. He suggested that Sarah should be given whisky and milk to drink.

William said that he would look after his wife but, whether on the doctor's suggestion or not, Chalkley arrested him the same afternoon, asking Susannah Liddington, the wife of the paper-maker, to look after Sarah. She and another neighbour, Louisa Swallow, sat up with the poor woman but she died in the early hours of Wednesday morning.

William was brought before the West Riding magistrates the same day charged with killing his wife.

An inquest was held on Sarah, again on the Wednesday, at the *New Inn* where the foreman of the jury was Thomas Robert Maddison of Dirtcar House, the manager of Woolley Well Main Colliery. Sarah's niece, Mrs Richard Hartley, the wife of a Kirkgate cordwainer, identified her aunt's body. Dr Andrew Thompson said that a post-mortem had found a large quantity of congealed blood in the brain tissue and that three large blood clots had been the immediate cause of death. He referred to the thickening of some of the skull bone and suggested that this would have impaired Sarah's intellect. The jury reached a unanimous verdict of manslaughter.

A further hearing before the magistrates led to William being committed to Leeds Assizes on the capital charge of murder. The case was heard on 15 May. Henry Clarke, the doctor at Wakefield Prison, gave evidence that, however wrong he might have been, Whittlestone was firmly convinced of his wife's adultery although this scarcely justified his actions. He was given eight years penal servitude.

Chapter 39

# It is Your Turn to Die
# 1890

**S**o said John Cottrell as he put a pistol to his friend John Holloway's head on Monday evening, 7 July 1890, and pulled the trigger. He meant it in fun. But the pistol was loaded.

Cottrell and Holloway had come to Wakefield the previous Wednesday for the summer fair. They worked for Holloway's cousin, William Edward Holloway, a showman who brought a booth with a tank in which Cottrell gave swimming exhibitions, and the Juvenile Twinkling Star swings. Cottrell

**Figure 49.** *The market area in Wakefield showing some fairground caravans parked to the left of the market hall.* Wakefield Historical Publications.

was seventeen and was William Holloway's brother-in-law. John Holloway was twenty-two and had married a couple of years earlier whilst in Ashton-under-Lyne. The group lived in caravans which, at the time of the fair, were parked close together on land adjoining Teall Street.

Cottrell and John Holloway were good friends and Cottrell was said to have been instrumental in securing better wages for his friend from their employer, William, obtaining a rise from twenty-one shillings a week to twenty-seven shillings.

Cottrell had bought the gun in Manchester after someone had tried to break into his van. But another showman, James Hutin, had shown an interest in buying it and on the fatal morning he, Cottrell and Holloway had looked at it together. It was a large-bore pistol with five chambers. Cottrell loaded it and gave a demonstration to the other two.

The fairground shows did not operate until Monday evening. In the afternoon Cottrell and Holloway went swimming at the baths in Almshouse Lane. Cottrell paid for them both and treated his friend to a drink afterwards on the way back to the fairground. Later in the afternoon Holloway brought out a small hatchet and began to shape a piece of wood into a chock to put beneath one of the wheels of his van.

And that was when Cottrell brought out the revolver again and – apparently forgetting that he had not emptied all the chambers, or perhaps not realising that the gun held more than one bullet – fired at Holloway. He probably died instantly. Cottrell rushed to Holloway's wife declaring, 'Fanny, I did not do it on purpose'. Police Inspectors Wright and Newton were quickly on the scene with Constable Illingworth. Wright arrested Cottrell while the others removed the body.

Cottrell was charged with manslaughter and brought before the Assizes at Leeds on 2 August. There the judge told the jury that there 'could not be any doubt that the prisoner was innocent of any intention to kill Holloway'. The jury never left the box but found him not guilty immediately.

## Chapter 40

# Released from the Asylum 1896

**I**f only he had not been released from the Pauper Lunatic Asylum!

In June 1895 William Moore, a quarryman living at 4 Stonedale Terrace, Snydale Road, Normanton, had made a savage attack on his wife. He had been found to be insane and was committed to the West Riding Pauper Lunatic Asylum in Wakefield (later Stanley Royd Hospital). Six months later he was held to have been cured and on Friday, 17 January 1896, he was discharged. His wife, Annie, and his sister, Catherine Newton, went from Normanton to bring him home. On the way they called at the house of Elsie Hall, Annie's aunt, in South Street, close to Kirkgate Station, where Annie confessed to her that she was afraid of what William might do to her. Her fears were well founded.

The couple had been married some fourteen years and had five children. Annie was thirty-two and William 'about' thirty-five. But the marriage was, it was said, not a happy one.

Even before the trio reached Normanton, William seems to have been talking strangely. The following evening Annie was so alarmed that she called at Normanton Police Station to alert the officers to her sense of danger. During the weekend the Moore children and the family's two lodgers must have been about but on Monday morning the former went to school and the latter to work. Annie and William were left alone. It was then, at about 9.30am, that a neighbour, Ellen Windroff, heard a terrible screaming. Her son, Thomas William, a coal miner, leapt over the fence that divided the gardens and got into the Moores' house. William was attacking Annie with a poker, striking her skull repeatedly. Thomas tried to drag her outside but William turned on him. Somehow Annie managed to crawl into the garden but William returned to the attack. Then he went back into the house. Annie was carried to a neighbour's and Dr Stewart was called. She was taken to Clayton Hospital in what must have been a terrible journey, in a cab and was admitted, unconscious at 1.40pm. She had a compound fracture of the skull and died without ever gaining consciousness.

An inquest at the hospital, under Coroner Thomas Taylor, brought a verdict of wilful murder against Moore. Annie was buried at Wakefield Cemetery on Friday 24 January. But Moore had disappeared. It seems that he went, on foot, begging for food and sleeping rough, to Pontefract and Doncaster and – or so he later said – to Retford, Newark, Grantham and Stamford before making his way back to Derbyshire where he presented himself at the home in Smalley Mill, near Chesterfield, of a former workmate from the Snydale quarries. The local police were quickly alerted and on the morning of 31 January, Inspector Akeroyd and Constable Taylor arrested him. He was found in his friend's home bathing his feet which were one mass of blisters. He asked the Inspector if his wife had died and if she had been buried and then broke down and wept. Inspector Akeroyd brought Moore back to Wakefield by train the same day. As the train made a prolonged stop at Walton, Moore, who had lost a stone in weight and was shivering with cold, was taken to sit by the fire in the waiting room where news spread of his presence and local people came to gaze at him. A crowd was awaiting his arrival at Westgate Station but the police escorted him swiftly down the steps to Westgate and into a waiting cab.

On 14 February, Moore was charged at the West Riding Police Court with murder and was committed for trial at the spring Assizes in Leeds. At the formal opening of the Assizes on 10 March, the judge, Henry Collins, referred to the case and observed that the mental condition of the prisoner was a most material element. Moore appeared  on 13 March. Evidence of his state of mind was given by Dr Bevan Lewis of the Pauper Lunatic Asylum and by Dr Henry Clarke of Wakefield prison. Both affirmed that he was suffering from delusions. The jury accepted that he had killed his wife but that he was not responsible for his actions. The judge ruled that he should be detained during Her Majesty's pleasure.

## Chapter 41

# The Waterworks Yard Murder 1905

I t must have been gravely distressing for Wakefield Councillor Thomas C Tattershall when, on Monday 3 July 1905, his thirty-one year old son murdered his (the son's) pregnant wife.

Thomas George Tattershall had married Rebecca Stead, the daughter of a Zetland Street tailor, in 1894. The couple lived initially in Red Lion Yard but had moved several times – to Pincheon Street and Dickinson's Yard among other places – before taking a cottage in Waterworks Yard in 1904. They had had eight children, four of whom had died. At the time of Rebecca's murder the four surviving children, who were all at home when their mother was killed, were Elizabeth Laura, aged ten, George (five), Edward (three) and Thomas (eighteen months).

Thomas, a plasterer by trade, was notorious as a drunkard and for habitually – and not infrequently violently – quarrelling with his wife. Little Laura had many times run to Holliday's Yard, Eastmoor, for her uncle, Charles Edward Stead, a general labourer, to come and intervene. She had done so only two days before the murder occurred.

But on Sunday evening 2 July, Thomas had seemed sober. His wife had seen the three older children to bed and then, cradling the toddler in her arms, had gone down the Yard to visit a neighbour. By the time she returned home Thomas too had gone to bed. She joined him. About 6.40am the next morning Laura was woken by a strange sound. She saw her father preparing to leave the house. His last words were a threat to kill her if she screamed.

Laura went to her parents' bedroom. What she saw was horrific. Her mother's throat was severed and she was bleeding profusely. She was still alive. Laura rushed into the Yard

**Figure 50.** *The scene of the Waterworks Yard murder as depicted in a contemporary newspaper report.* Peter Wood.

screaming. The cries were heard by a window cleaner, Arnold Harrison Heaton, of Robson's Yard, who was just then working on the windows of Hagenbach's shop in Northgate. He went to the cottage and found little George crying out, 'My dada has cut my mamma'. Eaton called out for help and John Broadbent went to the police station bringing back Police Sergeant Charles Stead (the similarity in names is coincidental). Dr Lionel Thomas Wells, who lived in Bond Street, was sent for but Rebecca, who had a four-and-a-half inch cut to the throat, was by then dead.

An inquest the following day brought a verdict of wilful murder against Tattershall. For a very short period it was thought that Tattershall might have committed suicide; he had been seen shortly after the murder walking along Denby Dale Road towards the river. However, as passengers from a train from Manchester alighted at Kirkgate Station on the Tuesday evening, the station-master, Oldham, recognised Tattershall among them. Railway Constable Firth arrested him and, with Constable Greenfield, called a hansom cab to take him to the police station. Thomas was brought before the magistrates the following morning and remanded in custody. At a further hearing, on 18 July, Thomas was committed for trial at Leeds Assizes. The case was heard on Saturday, 29 July. The jury brought in a verdict of guilty the same day and Thomas was hanged at Armley Gaol at 9.00am on 15 August.

Rebecca's funeral took place on at Wakefield Cemetery and was conducted by Reverend W H Noble, a curate at Wakefield Cathedral.

Immediately after their mother's murder, the children were taken into the care of their maternal grandmother, who lived in Library Yard, Northgate. But shortly afterwards Laura, and perhaps the others too, went to live with Thomas's father at Thornhill House, Trinity Church Gate.

## Chapter 42

# A Domestic Tragedy at Lupset 1930

A foolish act at work led to the tragic and macabre deaths in the summer of 1930 of twenty-eight year old Ernest Taylor Bousfield, his wife, Elizabeth (Cissie) Victoria, also twenty-eight, and two of their three children..

The Bousfields had moved into 24 George-a-Green Road, on the new Lupset housing estate, some eighteen months earlier. Mr Bousfield's sister and brother-in-law, Mr and Mrs Harold Webb, lived close by, in Haselden Road, and Cissie's widowed mother had also come to live at Lupset, at 1 Hall Road, Snapethorpe. They were regarded as a happy family. The day before the dreadful events, Cissie Bousfield had taken her eight-year old daughter, Margaret, to the Sunday School anniversary at the Primitive Methodist Chapel on Dewsbury Road.

But Bousfield worked as a driver for the Wakefield Borough Co-operative Society and had been found to have stolen some of the Society's goods. He had returned these but on the Saturday evening before the tragedy he had been suspended and told not to come in to work again until he had met members of the Society's committee the following Tuesday.

Bousfield may have already been prone to depression. Two of his brothers had died in the First World War and this seems to have preyed on his mind. Then a year or two before the tragedy, when he was working as a motor mechanic for Tate's, he had taken part in a particularly unpleasant practical joke. He and a colleague had had to take one of the firm's vehicles to Dewsbury and they had telegraphed back with the words 'Accident. Driver killed'. His recollection of the earlier stupidity may have contributed to his state of mind on the fatal night.

**Figure 51.** *Houses in George-a-Green Road, Lupset. The Bousfields lived in the left hand house of the semi-detached pair in the centre of the picture.*

On Monday morning, 26 May, the Bousfields' neighbour, Mrs Mercy Beatrice Causebrook, realised there must be something wrong next door. Her mother, Rose Wilde, who lived with her, reported hearing a groan or moan about three o'clock in the morning. At nine am the milk boy asked Mrs Causebrook to take in the Bousfields' milk as he could get no reply from their house. Mrs Causebrook's husband, Thomas, returning from his shift as a driver with the West Riding

Automobile Company, noticed that the Bousfields' blinds were still closed. He went round to the home of the Webbs and Harold, who was also a West Riding bus driver, returned with him to the Bousfields. They found the door open and, finding no response to their calls, made their way upstairs. In one room lay Cissie with her two-year old son Harold in a cot beside her. In the other, lay Margaret and four-year old Kenneth. All were unconscious and all had serious head wounds. There was a bloodstained axe on the staircase. Of Bousfield himself there was no sign. The police and ambulances were summoned and the mother and children were taken to Clayton Hospital. Both boys died later that day without regaining consciousness.

Meanwhile John Mills, of Tadman's Buildings, had noticed a cap and coat by the side of Jessop's Lock on the Aire and Calder Navigation at Durkar. He reported the discovery to the police. They found the body of Bousfield in the water.

Inquests were opened the following day in Wakefield Town Hall. It fell to Bousfield's father, Fred Bousfield, a fish-and-chip fryer of 63 Northgate, Wakefield, to identify the bodies of his son and two grandchildren. And it was Fred's lot also to arrange the funeral. After a short service at Fred's house, conducted by Reverend Edward C Hamer, the curate of the new Lupset ecclesiastical district, Bousfield and the boys were buried in the same grave at Wakefield cemetery.

The inquest resumed the following Tuesday, 3 June, when the jury found that the boys had been killed by their father and that he had taken his own life whilst temporarily insane. Cissie died the next day, without regaining consciousness and on 4 June a further inquest found that she, too, had been killed by Bousfield.

Whether Margaret made a recovery is not known by the present writer.

## Chapter 43

# A Woman with a Dreadful Secret 1941

When thirty-three year old Winifred Mary Hallaghan was arrested for stealing £130 from Walton post office in 1946 she readily pleaded guilty. Perhaps she really had stolen the money. But no one at the time knew that she had already done something much more terrible and it may be that she admitted to the theft just to avoid too many questions being asked. She was brought before the West Riding magistrates on 18 June when her good character was stressed and the case was adjourned to allow time for her to repay the money. When she returned to court on 12 August she had already repaid £65 and she was bound over for two years.

The case was recalled when Winifred appeared at the Leeds Assizes on 9 March 1949 charged with the manslaughter of her great aunt eight years previously, and with forgery.

Winifred had for some years as a child lived in Wakefield with her great aunt, Emma Eliza Sheard, the widow of a coachman, and after she was married to Don in 1932 she and her husband had spent a further year at her aunt's house. They had then moved into their own home at 4 Chevet Terrace, Walton, close to Sharlston West Colliery.

When war broke out in 1939, the Hallaghans invited Emma Sheard to stay with them, thinking that she might be nervous on her own. But Mrs Sheard was not an easy woman to have about the house. Early in 1941 there was a silly quarrel between the old lady and Don Hallaghan over a light bulb. He had changed the living room bulb from a 60 watt one to a 100 watt one and she had accused him of swapping it with the one in her bedroom. The quarrel ended with his saying that she must go.

Some while later there had been further 'words' between Winifred Hallaghan and her aunt. Her aunt said that it was

**Figure 52.** *Walton Post Office in 2001*

Don who should go, not her, because he was 'carrying on' with the woman next door. Winifred did not for a moment believe her but she was sufficiently angered by her aunt's foul tongue that she hit her. According to Winifred's later evidence, her great aunt fell backwards, striking her head against the corner of the sewing machine. She left her there. Returning some hours later she found her great aunt still lying there and with foam about her mouth. She dragged her to her bed already suspecting that the old woman was, in fact, dead.

What happened next is, again, known only from Winifred's own confession. She meant to tell her husband what had happened and ran towards the pit. But she then noticed children playing round a capped shaft some hundred yards from her home. And it occurred to her that she could neatly pop the dead woman down the shaft and no one need know. Her younger child was only eighteen months old and visions of having to leave him for the prison cell must have terrified her. That night she put the body in the baby's pram and wheeled it to the shaft, removed the shaft cover and dropped her aunt down wrapped in a blanket.

And there Emma Sheard remained.

Of course questions were asked but Winifred simply said that her aunt had left – at her husband's bidding – and she did not know where she had gone. Winifred's mother was hard to satisfy and, at her request, Winifred called at the police station in Wood Street, Wakefield, and reported her great aunt missing.

Mrs Sheard owned a cottage in Neville Street, Belle Vue, and was in the habit of calling on her tenant each week to collect the rent. But Winifred continued to collect it herself. Then in 1943 she decided to sell the property. She explained to Ralph Sweeting, the solicitor that acted on her behalf and to whom she brought the title deeds, that Mrs Sheard was not well enough to come into Wakefield herself but that she would take the deed of conveyance home and get her to sign it there. In fact she signed it herself in Mrs Sheard's name. The cottage was sold for £300 and Winifred pocketed the £294 14s 9d that was left after Sweeting had taken his fee.

Winifred lived for years with the her aunt's wretched fate

known only to herself. The shaft had been disused from the time of its first sinking when an inrush of water had led to its being abandoned. It seems that in 1946 she told her husband and her brother, James Arthur Foster, a joiner of Boldon Colliery, County Durham, what had happened but they kept her secret.

Eventually, however, the crime - whatever it precisely was - came to light. On 16 December 1948 a colliery electrician was sent to inspect the disused shaft.

He saw a body lying 126 feet below the surface. The following day a headless torso was raised on an improvised cradle. The head had fallen off as it was being moved. On 18 December Winifred was questioned by Police Sergeant Joseph Glendenning about the whereabouts of her aunt. Winifred insisted that, after a quarrel with her husband, Mrs Sheard had left. Three days later members of the Mines Rescue Service were engaged to search the shaft. Within minutes of their being lowered in an iron hopper, they brought out items of clothing and more body parts. Two days before Christmas, Sergeant Glendenning called on Winifred again and took her to the police station where she was questioned by Detective Chief Superintendent John Wallace. Initially she maintained her original story, that her aunt had left after a quarrel, but persistent questioning led to the admission that her aunt had fallen when she had hit her and that three hours later she had found her dead. She was charged with murder and remanded in custody.

It was not until 31 January that Mrs Sheard's head was recovered.

Meanwhile the police were making further enquiries. When Winifred appeared before the magistrates on 3 February 1949 the charges included uttering a forged conveyance and obtaining money by means of forgery. Winifred's solicitor, T Vernon Way, argued that there was not enough evidence to substantiate a charge of murder. She was committed for trial at the Assizes on the lesser charge of manslaughter.

Dressed in a dark blue mackintosh, a dark blue hat and black gloves, Winifred was tried at Leeds Assizes on 9 March 1949. She pleaded guilty to the crime of manslaughter and to three

**Figure 53.** *Chevet Terrace, Walton. Winifred Hallaghan lived at number 4.*

charges of forgery. Sentence was deferred until 14 March when she was given five years penal servitude for the acts of forgery and three years for manslaughter. The judge commented that he regarded the forgeries as the more serious acts. Perhaps, indeed, they were the more deliberate ones.

## Chapter 44

# The Wakefield Chorister Turned Serial Killer, 1944-49

By 1949 John George Haigh must have believed that he really could get away with murder. It seems that he was never even questioned in connection with the five (at least) deaths for which he had been responsible in the previous five years. But in the case of the sixty-nine year old widow, Mrs Olivia Helen Henrietta Olive Robarts Durand-Deacon, whom he murdered on 18 February 1949, he was too obvious a suspect for the police to ignore. At his trial at the Sussex Assizes at Lewes in July 1949 his defending counsel argued that Haigh was insane and that his paranoia could be traced to his unhappy childhood in Wakefield and to his parents' religious adherence.

Haigh was born in Stamford on 24 July 1909 but the family moved to Grange View, Ledger Lane, Outwood when his father, John Robert Haigh, obtained work at Lofthouse Colliery. His parents were for a time members of the Plymouth Brethren, a fundamentalist sect opposed to any kind of indulgence or pleasure to be derived from this-world activities. Haigh is said to have been treated very strictly and deprived of the companionship of other children. If he was already confused, matters may well have got worse when his parents adopted a very different high-church outlook and encouraged him to try for a choral scholarship which assured him a place, at the age of seven, at the Queen Elizabeth Grammar School and training in Wakefield Cathedral choir.

Haigh's problem seems to have been less insanity than an inability to work hard and earn his own living. He failed his school certificate and drifted from working as a motor mechanic to an office job before starting his own business when he was twenty-one. In 1934 he was tried at Leeds Assizes for fraud and forgery and served his first spell in prison. Two

**Figure 54.** *Ledger Lane, Outwood, where serial killer John George Haigh lived as a boy.*

similar convictions followed.

By 1944 Haigh was living in London in a basement flat at 79 Gloucester Road. Here, if his confession is to be believed, he committed the first of his murders. He made the acquaintance of a young man named William Donald McSwann, lured him to his flat, killed him with a blow and disposed of his body by immersing it in a container of acid. He told McSwann's parents, Donald and Amy, that their son had gone away to avoid being called up for military service. He maintained the fiction by sending letters to the McSwanns, purporting to be from William, from Glasgow and Edinburgh. Some months later he invited the McSwanns to Gloucester Road and killed them both, again immersing their bodies in acid.

Haigh claimed, when he recounted his exploits to the police, that in each case he made an incision in his victim's neck and drank a glassful of blood but it may well be that this ghastly admission was simply a ruse to convince the police and the trial judge that he was mad.

Haigh's fatal acqaintance with Dr Archibald Henderson and his wife, Rosaline, began when the couple advertised their home at 22 Ladbroke Grove, London, for sale. He struck up a friendship with them and visited them at their new house, 16 Dawes Road, Fulham, when they were staying at Kingsgate Castle in Kent and again, in 1948, when they were at the Metropole in Brighton. By now Haigh had access to a storeroom in Crawley which belonged to the firm of Hurstlea Products and which he was able to use to 'conduct experiments'. From Brighton he took Dr Henderson 'to see the storeroom' and, once there, shot him with his own revolver which Haigh had stolen from the Dawes Road house. He then fetched Mrs Henderson, telling her that her husband had been taken ill, shot her too and disposed of both bodies by his now familiar acid-bath technique. He claimed to have again performed the ritual of the incision in the neck and the drinking of blood. He used the Hendersons' own money to pay their hotel bill, collected their red-setter dog and removed their luggage, leaving it back at Dawes Road. Later he forged documents and sold the Hendersons' house to one J B Clarke. He kept the dog himself for some time before sending it to kennels.

In early 1949 Haigh was staying in the *Onslow Court Hotel*, South Kensington. He sat at the next table to the widow who was to be his next victim. In February 1949 he was being pressed by the hotel to pay the arrears on his bill, he had an £80 overdraft at the bank and he owed Mr Jones, the managing director of Hurstlea Products, some £50.

Mrs Durand-Deacon spoke of wanting some plastic fingernails. Haigh assured her that he knew of a firm that would make them. He set about buying some red cellophane, for the nails, together with thirty gallons of sulphuric acid, a stirrup pump, gloves and an apron. Then he invited his victim to go with him to Crawley. The pair left Onslow Court in Haigh's car on 18 February, she wearing a Persian lamb coat. They were seen together at a hotel in Crawley between 4.00pm and 5.00pm. At 6.30pm Haigh was seen alone in a restaurant in Crawley where he had some poached eggs on toast. Between 5.00pm and 6.30pm he had shot Mrs Durand-Deacon at the storeroom and taken her coat, the jewellery she was wearing and the valuables she had in her handbag. After his tea he returned to the storeroom and began the customary process of dissolving the widow's body, putting it in a drum and filling the drum with acid.

The following day Haigh asked another resident at Onslow Court, a Mrs Lane, with every show of concern, whether she had seen Mrs Durand-Deacon and whether she was perhaps ill. He then returned to Crawley and sold Mrs Durand-Deacon's watch for £10 giving his name as Miller.

On 20 February, Mrs Lane told Haigh that she thought she ought to report Mrs Durand-Deacon's disappearance to the police. Haigh went with her.

But of course it was known that two days earlier it was with Haigh that the missing woman had left the hotel. On 21 February the police questioned Haigh for the first time. Yes, he said, he had indeed taken the widow by car from the hotel but they had stopped at the Army and Navy Stores where she wanted to do some shopping. That was the last time he had seen her. He returned to pick her up at the appointed time but she never appeared.

After the police had gone, Haigh went back to Crawley to see how far the acid had dissolved the body. Some of the human remains were still very visible. He poured out some of the 'used' acid and refilled the drum. He went back again the next day and emptied the drum onto earth outside the storehouse. What Haigh may not have realised was that something of the body was still identifiable in the slurry.

Haigh was questioned by the police again on 24 February. They searched the storeroom in Crawley and found the carboys of acid, the revolver and some bullets, rubber gloves, the red cellophane and a receipt for a fur coat from a dry cleaners in Reigate. They were also able to establish that Haigh had sold items of Mrs Durand-Deacon's jewellery. The police then confronted Haigh with the evidence they had obtained. He did not deny the murder but challenged them saying, 'She no longer exists. She has disappeared completely. I have destroyed her with acid. How can you prove murder if there is no body?' He was told that some of the body still remained. He then made a statement admitting the crime and adding that he had cut his victim's neck and drunk a glass of her blood.

Now Haigh volunteered an account of the five murders he had previously committed. The police would find all the relevant documentation, he said, in a file in his room at Onslow Court.

Haigh was interviewed again, in Lewes prison, on 4 March. This time he told the police of three further murders he had committed, those of a young woman whom he had met in Hammersmith, a young man he had met in the *Goat* public house, and a girl called Mary whom he had encountered at Eastbourne. Perhaps this latest confession was pure fabrication. If so it may well have been because Haigh wished to convince the police that he was mad.

Haigh was tried only on the charge of murdering Mrs Durand-Deacon. The prosecuting barrister was no less a figure than Sir Hartley Shawcross, the Attorney-General. Acting for Haigh was Sir David Maxwell Fyfe who said that the defence would be directed to showing that Haigh was insane; driven mad by his childhood terror of his parents' religion and suffering from appalling nightmares in which he saw forests of crucifixes which turned into trees.

The trial lasted only two days. The chief witness was a consultant psychiatrist, Dr Henry Yellowlees. He described

Haigh as verbose, egocentric, without either shame or remorse and quite unable to tell the truth, in short suffering from paranoia. Shawcross countered by suggesting that Haigh was quite clever enough to deceive the specialist.

The jury took a mere fifteen minutes to reach a guilty verdict and the judge passed the death sentence.

Haigh was subsequently examined by further experts but they found no grounds for recommending a reprieve. On 10 August 1949 he was executed at Wandsworth prison.

## Chapter 45

# He Could Not Get On
# With His Father, 1957

**T**wenty-year old George Robinson-Brannan's efforts in August 1957 to persuade staff at the Wakefield branch of the Halifax Building Society that his father's investment should be transferred to him led to his arrest and the discovery of his father's body hidden in a clothes cupboard at their home in Denby Dale Road, Wakefield.

Robinson-Brannan was in some ways a pathetic figure. Short of stature and with his fair hair already receding, he seemed unable to hold down a job or to maintain any permanent relationship with his homosexual partners. His mother, who had been profoundly distressed by his sexual disposition, had died when he was sixteen and, when in a cantankerous mood, his father taunted him with causing her death. He had formed a heterosexual relationship in his late teens and the girl had become pregnant, but his father would not consent to their marriage.

Robinson-Brannan met Laurence Albert Avery when he was working as a hotel porter in Leeds in April 1957. Avery stayed overnight at least once at his friend's home but Robinson-Brannan's father, William Robinson, made his view of his son's friendship quite clear. Robinson-Brannan moved over to Hull, where Avery lived, in May and took a job in a hotel there but he quarreled with Avery over the payment of rent and Avery threw him out.

Back in Wakefield, Robinson-Brannan took a job as a copy typist with Bituminous Compositions, remaining in their employment until 26 July. While he was there a couple of cheques went missing. It was later discovered that Robinson-Brannan had managed to cash one, made out for £2 15s, at the local grocer's shop, 40 Denby Dale Road which was kept by Irene and Edwin Binns.

On 21 July William Robinson, who was seventy, was injured, in somewhat mysterious circumstances, and admitted to Clayton Hospital. It seems that his son took the opportunity to help himself to some hospital notepaper for Avery received a letter purporting to be from the hospital matron, urging him to be kind to his former friend.

Avery relented and came over to Wakefield, staying at Robinson-Brannan's home on 26 July. There he was shown bloodstains and told that the old man had been knocked down by a car.

William Robinson was discharged from hospital on 7 August and examined, at home, by Dr Knowles. It was the last time that anyone other than his son saw him alive.

Out of work again, Robinson-Brannan was by now short of money. At some point, on or about 19 August, he attempted to sell a gold watch to a Wakefield jeweller, Mr Holmes. Holmes requested proof of ownership and Robinson-Brannan returned with his father's will, explaining to the jeweller that his father had died. He obtained £7.

But then the young man took the more ambitious step which was to lead to his arrest. He went to see the chief clerk at the Halifax Building Society, a Mr Ingham, and told him that his father was about to enter an old people's home and that, if the old man were to receive financial support, he would need to divest himself of his assets. Robinson-Brannan asked that the £310 in his father's account be transferred to himself. He produced two letters, supposedly from his father, confirming that he wanted the money to go to his son. The address on the letters was 4 Alpha Terrace, Hull - Avery's address. Ingham was very suspicious and, explaining that the signatures on the letters were unlike the specimens the Society held, he refused the request. Brannan-Robinson returned with a letter purporting to be from Dr O'Neill of Hull and verifying the fact that William Robinson's signature had changed. Ingham was not suprised when he contacted Dr O'Neill and found that he denied all knowledge of any such letter. He referred the whole matter to the police.

Meanwhile on 23 August another young man, Barry Fraser, came to stay with Robinson-Brannan in Denby Dale Road. He

**Figure 55.** *The shop in Denby Dale Road where George Robinson-Brannan asked for something to take away bad smells.*

remarked on a bad smell in the house and was told by his host that it was a problem with the drains. Fraser was later to give evidence that he had seen Robinson-Brannan stuffing rags round a door leading from one of the bedrooms and nailing the door up. Fraser noticed a red scarf and Robinson-Brannan said to him, 'That's what I tried to strangle the old bugger with one of the times we had a row.' The unpleasant smell remained and Robinson-Brannan asked shopkeeper Edwin Binns to sell him a spray that would counter it. On 29 August, according to Fraser, Robinson-Brannan sold a quantity of garments to an old-clothes merchant.

On 31 August Detective Inspector K Oakley and Detective Officer A Kirk called at the house to ask Robinson-Brannan about his request to the building society. The young man repeated his story that his father was about to enter a residential home but the officers were far from convinced. It seemed clear that, at the very least, there had been an attempt to obtain money by false pretences. A search of the house unearthed some postal orders, and another cheque belonging to Bituminous Compositions. Robinson-Brannan was arrested on a charge of larceny and taken into custody. It was discovered much later that he had forged a number of documents in order to obtain his father's state pension and his pension from the Spencer Wire Company.

The following day, Sunday 1 September, Oakley and Kirk searched the house. The smell of decay was pervasive. They found the nailed-up door and got it open. Behind it, in what was a clothes closet, lay a partly decomposed body. It was removed on a stretcher through the window of the front bedroom and taken to the mortuary. The body was identified by William Brannan, of Canal Lane, Stanley, as that of William Robinson. The remains were examined by consultant pathologist D E Price, who was able to say that the death had occurred about the middle of August and was due to asphyxia following manual strangulation. An inquest was opened on 2 September and was adjourned pending criminal proceedings. Robinson-Brannan was charged with the murder.

After a series of remands, including one occasion when Robinson-Brannan was said to be too ill with 'flu to appear in court, the case was heard before Wakefield magistrates on 29 October and he was committed for trial at Leeds Assizes.

At the Assizes, in the middle of December, it was said that the friction between father and son had worsened when Robinson discovered that the young man had obtained £14 8s 11d by forging his signature on some of his savings certificates. He was accused of seeing his father as a barrier between himself and his father's money and of seeking to rob his brother and half-brother of the share left to them in Robinson's will.

In Robinson-Brannan's defence much was made of Robinson's harsh treatment of his son and his cantankerous disposition. The killing had not been premeditated but occurred as a result of a quarrel on 9 August when Robinson had told his son that he was not to go out until he had handed over £3 5s for his board. Robinson-Brannan claimed that his father had then hit him with a strap, called him a bastard and brought up his sexual relationship with Avery. He was in love with the Hull man and could not bear to hear him disparaged. He accepted that he had strangled his father but had not meant to kill him.

Nonetheless Robinson-Brannan was found guilty of murder and was sentenced to life imprisonment.

## Chapter 46

# Murder at the ABC Steps 1965

**D**isastrously the jury at the inquest into the death of fourteen-year old Elsie Frost on 9 October 1965 not only found that she had been unlawfully killed but named her killer despite police evidence that their investigations were far from complete and no arrest was imminent. The coroner then, following traditional practice, committed the named individual for trial at the West Riding Assizes and the police had no option but to arrest him. Not surprisingly, at an interim hearing before Wakefield magistrates, the defence counsel observed that the inquest system was 'an archaic institution whose demise is sought by many'.

The evidence against thirty-three year old railway fireman Ian Bernard Spencer of Thornes Lane, who was married and had a young son, was never more than circumstantial.

Elsie Frost, of Manor Haigh Road, Lupset, was one of a number of teenage boys and girls who were accustomed to sail at Millfield Lagoon, Horbury. They were supervised by local schoolteachers including Ronald Joseph Way and John Blackburn. Spencer, who had his own canoe, enjoyed assisting at the lagoon and had built a jetty there. Elsie has been described by a former neighbour as 'more than an ordinarily likable child' who 'stood out conspicuously with her charm and liveliness'.

On the day of her death Elsie had left home about 1.30pm and arrived at the lagoon, on foot, about 2.00pm. She left again at about 4.00pm and her body was found towards the bottom of the ABC steps – on the route to and from her home – at about 4.23pm by Thomas Raymond Brown, and electrical engineer of Thornes Moor Road, who was taking his small children for a walk. He hurried back to a neighbour's house to

**Figure 56.** *Millfield lagoon, Horbury, where Elsie Frost used to go sailing.*

summon help. Elsie was also seen, at 4.25pm, by John Ewart
Hall, a sixteen year old pupil at Snapethorpe City High School
who was one of the sailing instructors at the lagoon.

The ABC steps form part of a pathway from Thornes Moor Road and lead down to an arch under the Wakefield – Huddersfield railway line and on to the towpath of the Calder and Hebble Navigation. A further path, from the same arch, runs parallel to the railway line and leads to the lagoon.

Forensic evidence suggested that Elsie had been attacked from behind. Five stab wounds included one which penetrated her heart. She had not been sexually molested and was still a virgin. Nothing had been stolen from her handbag or pockets. There was no apparent motive for the killing.

According to Brian Bedford, he had been at the ABC steps at about 3.50pm and saw nothing of Elsie. He was seen there by Kenneth Garbutt when he was exercising his Alsatian and he, too, had seen nothing of the girl.

Evidently Elsie had been killed between Bedford's leaving the steps and John Hall finding her there dead. Much hinged on where Spencer had been at the critical time. Spencer himself said initially that he had finished work at five past two, called at his home to change into his black reefer jacket and wellington boots, and gone to the lagoon to check whether some timber he had taken to use on his jetty was still there. He had arrived at the lagoon about 2.55pm. He was there for five minutes or so and had a brief chat with Ronald Way, the schoolmaster-instructor. Whilst he was there he had seen Way adjust the rigging on one of the dinghies. He reached home again at 3.30pm. In a second statement he admitted that whilst he was at home at lunchtime he had had a meal and that on his way to the lagoon he had talked to two lads, Richard Jackson and Gerald Burton, at the Bon Bon shop in Thornes Road. He still insisted, however, that he had reached the lagoon by 3.00pm and was home again at 3.30pm. At about 4.00pm he asked his young son, Lee, whether he wanted to watch wrestling on television but then realised that it had been on already for some time and went to have a bath instead. His wife and a friend of hers had been in the house all the time from 3.30pm until they went out about 6.15pm.

But other people reported seeing Spencer at rather different times. The two boys, Richard Jackson and Gerald Burton, said it had been three o'clock when they met Spencer at the Bon

**Figure 57.** *The ABC steps where Elsie Frost's body was found.*

Bon. Undertaker Jack Shillito had also spoken to Spencer outside the Bon Bon and he, too, confirmed that it had been at 3.00pm. One of the girls in the sailing group, Penelope Gillies, thought that Spencer had been at the lagoon at about 3.15pm or 3.30pm. Ronald Way thought he had talked to Spencer briefly at the lagoon at about 3.00pm but that it was at the time that a group of three students were having difficulty with their sail. All three were sure that the time of that incident was 3.30pm rather than 3.00pm. Frank Robson, an engineer living in Major Street, was convinced that he had seen Spencer at the junction of Secker Street and Vernon Place at half past four.

But there was nothing vague in the statement of ABC Television's logging clerk that the wrestling programme that Saturday afternoon had not begun until two minutes past four, thus it could hardly have been on for some time, as Spencer averred, at four o'clock. There had been a commercial break at 4.11pm and then the wrestling had continued until 4.27pm.

Elsie had been stabbed with a knife. Dr Donald Hainsworth, who carried out a post-mortem examination of Elsie's body, concluded that the knife which had been used would have had a blade of at least four inches in length and which would have tapered sharply to its point. Shown a sheath knife, he confirmed that it was comparable to the one use to kill her. A sheath was found on waste land between Holme Lane and Denby Dale Road on 13 October by Jack Swain. It was identified by a commercial traveller as one marketed with a its knife by Whitby and Co of Kendal; it was quite a new line and it would have been obtainable from Holdsworth's, in Wood Street, Wakefield, from May 1965. One of Spencer's colleagues recalled his having a sheath knife but, although several knives were found at Spencer's home, none fitted the forensic description. Elsie's wounds had bled extensively but no blood was found on any of Spencer's clothing except a spot on a pair of trousers which was not of the same blood group as Elsie's. There was no blood on his bicycle or on his knives or knife sheath.

The verdict of the inquest jury that there was a *prima facie* case against Spencer gave the police no alternative but to arrest him and charge him with the murder. The hearing before Wakefield magistrates in February 1966 took five days and at the end of it they concluded that there was no case for Spencer to answer. However, because of the coroner's warrant, he had to remain in custody until the decision at Leeds Assizes. There on 10 March 1966 it took only a five-minute hearing for the case to be dropped and for Spencer to go free.

Elsie Frost's murder remains unavenged to this day.

# Sources

1. Printed volumes of the Wakefield Manor Court Rolls.
2. Thomas Taylor, *The History of Wakefield Rectory Manor*, 1886.
3. Anon. *A full and true relation of a most barbarous and cruel robbery and murder, committed by six men and one woman near Wakefield in Yorkshire*, 1677, in the Hailstone Collection, York Minster Library.
4. Copies of local and other newspapers including the *Times*, the *Wakefield Star*, the *Wakefield and Halifax Journal*, the *Wakefield and West Riding Herald*, the *Wakefield Express* and the *Leeds Mercury*.
5. Inquest books compiled by Thomas Taylor, West Yorkshire Archive Service.
6. Michael Clare and Catherine Crawford (eds), Legal Medicine in History, 1994.
7. Thomas R. Forbes, 'Crowner's Quest', *Transactions of the American Philosophical Society*, 1978.
8. A Lucas, *Forensic Chemistry*, 1935.
9. J P Howe, *The Badsworth Murder Case, by a Law Student*, 1888.
10. Brief of 1788 by David Colvard, in the John Goodchild Collection, Wakefield.
11. Ian Harley, *Black Barnsley*, 1999.
12. Barry Shaw, *Murderous Yorkshire*, 1980.
13. J Hewitt, *The History of Wakefield*, 1862.

# Foul Deeds
# and Suspicious Deaths Series

Foul Deeds and Suspicious Deaths on the
**Yorkshire Coast**

BY ALAN WHITWORTH

Mankind often demonstrates the full range of emotions, ranging from extreme gentleness, to the most brutal savagery, being capable of bringing to bear extremes of ferocity in attack or defence. Passion, in one form or another, is often the driving force behind this violence, be it in the form of love, hatred, fear or jealousy.

In *Foul Deeds and Suspicious Deaths on the Yorkshire Coast*, we encounter the unleashing of these passions and the deadly results of that release. From a Roman sentry stabbed in the back and his murderer lying dead beside him, his throat torn out by his victim's dog, to relatively modern murders of friends, loved ones, or hated rivals in love and business.

*...a fascinating insight into the less well known history of coastal Yorkshire.*

**1·903425·01·8  £9.99**

Newborough Bar, Scarborough, in the early nineteenth century. Criminals were often hung from this.

# INDEX

## INDEX OF PLACES